MW01602093

Raising The
Empowered Puppy,
Published By Jeanette Forrey

JEANETTE FORREY
RAISING THE EMPOWERED PUPPY FORREY JEANETTE

Library of Congress Control Number
ISBN:979-889074095-3

WWW.4EKENNELS.COM
WWW.BADASSBREEDER.COM
WWW.JEANETTEFORREY.COM
WWW.4EHEALINGHEARTS.COM

To my kids living at home while I was writing this book, Matthew, Jenna and Kae, this was a labor of love by not only me but you as well. You continue to have a parent that is "here" but not as present as I need to be. Your countless "fend for yourself" dinners and constantly tired mom has not been easy for you. Your sacrifices have not gone unnoticed, and I love you more than you could ever know.

To all the dogs in the world, this dedication is for each and every one of you, no matter how you came into our lives. You deserve honor, respect, and love throughout your journey. Whether bred responsibly or found in less-than-ideal circumstances, your worth is immeasurable. May you find compassionate humans who understand your needs and treat you with the care and respect you deserve. You are valued members of our families and cherished companions.

Your unwavering loyalty, unconditional love, and unique personalities enrich our lives beyond measure. We should strive to reciprocate the selflessness you show us. Let's ensure your needs are met, keep you safe from harm, and appreciate the incredible bond between dog and human.

Together, let's promote responsible pet ownership and breeding and treat all dogs with the love, compassion, and understanding they deserve. We *can* create a world where every dog is honored, respected, and loved.

With deep gratitude and a commitment to always do better.

For our breeders.
For our owners.
And most importantly for our dogs.

Love,
Jeanette

Welcome to the "Raising the Empowered Puppy" family! I am so glad you are here. My journey into the dog world started when I was a child. I was raised in a small town in Montana by a mom who loved babies. Human and animal alike. We almost always had a litter of kittens or puppies. No fence. No spay or neuter. We were a blue-collar family. My mom was a stay-at-home mom, and my dad worked at the local paper mill. We were nestled in the mountains with the Big Fork River snaking its way through the outskirts of town.

In our neighborhood, puppies traded hands like extra firewood or a cup of milk for a birthday cake recipe when the local grocery store was closed. Picked up from the front porch in a cardboard box, ready for their next adventure down the road. That is all I knew. I spent my childhood raising puppies of all types. Heinz 57-type dogs. Sometimes the best, right? I kept detailed spiral notebooks tracking their development. Their personalities. Their excitement and their fears. It was where I felt safest. Where I belonged.

When the puppies were weaned and ready to move on, I was eager to share all I had learned over the first few weeks of their life. Much to my dismay, people quite often did not care. They did not ask questions about their personality. What did they like? How did they play? Who was brave? Who wanted to be held all the time? There was so much I could have offered them to ensure my puppies were honored for their unique needs and that their new families were prepared to welcome them. My puppies did not have the voice that they so desperately needed. I was sad and frustrated.

So how did I get here? The short version?

In middle school, I checked out a book about Yorkshire Terriers from the library. I wanted one so badly. A purebred dog? Unheard of! My mom bought me one for my birthday. A breeder came to our house with several under her shirt (don't ask, I don't know) and let me pick one out. I was in heaven. My dreams came true. I loved that little thing so much. It was not long before she was pregnant with some neighborhood dog. We had puppies before. Many times before. I had witnessed the birth and raised puppies several times. But this delivery was far from ordinary. She was sick. We rushed her to the nearest vet clinic over 30 miles away. The vet said she needed a c-section and that I could help. She started handing me puppies. I cleared their airway, dried them off, and placed them in a box. We were delivering the fourth and last pup, and her heart stopped.

My dog's heart freaking stopped.

The vet performed CPR as I took care of the last puppy. Tears welled up in my eyes as I watched my dog die. She recommended the pups be euthanized. I grabbed the box, and my mom and I left.

It was a challenging learning experience. The pups were not warm enough. One died. One aspirated formula. Died. I don't even know why the third pup died, too. But one lived. One made it. My heart hurt, and I was unprepared and not ready emotionally, so we rehomed her.

My dad brought home a red golden retriever male that his coworker had to rehome. A beautiful adult golden retriever. I was in awe. His big brown eyes, his trainability, his heart. He would carry my sister's baby blanket around the house and "talk." I would forever be changed.

Years later, I left my small town and went to college. I had always had a dog and needed one, and college was no different. I hid Nala, a faithful mutt in all aspects of the word, in my dorm room for several weeks. When the semester ended, I moved back home. After graduating with a degree in secondary education, I moved to Las Vegas for a teaching job. Nala was by my side through the breakup of my seven-year relationship with my high school sweetheart, student teaching, first-year teaching, meeting my husband, and becoming an instant stepmom. She supported me through my new husband's custody battle, three years of infertility, a high-risk pregnancy, and finally, a baby. Nala died of pancreatitis when my son was an infant. She was only ten years old. We tried everything. We maxed out our only credit card and did several blood transfusions, but the vet told us they had done all they could. I was devastated. That dog knew me better than anyone. I called my brother as she lay dying in my arms late one night. He rushed over and sat with me as she took her last breaths.

After Nala's passing, I could not fathom loving another dog. She left a hole in my heart that I did not know how to fill. But, deep down, I knew my life was not complete without a dog. So, I started working with local rescues and rehabbing dogs that were given a final chance at life. My experience as a child gave me the confidence to work with challenging dogs, figure out how to honor their story and unique needs, and empower them to live happy and fulfilling lives. It was harrowing and heart-wrenching, but I learned a great deal about dog behavior and how much we have failed our canines. Between bad breeding and bad ownership, it was a disaster. I soon realized that playing "clean up" was not always as impactful as addressing the problems at the source, but I did not know where to start. So, temporarily, I kept bringing dogs into my life until we settled down with two dogs - Obi and Getzy. One a rescue and one a purebred toy poodle. What a motley crew!

I trained Getzy to be a therapy dog, and we visited long-term care facilities every Thursday night together. I loved therapy dog work and knew a dog's power to heal hearts and change lives. It did not take long before these Thursday nights were the highlight of my week. I found such joy in bringing the healing power of a dog to people who really needed it while also honoring the innate desire of Getzy to provide therapeutic support. I soon knew it was time to dream even bigger. I wanted to bring a dog into my 8th grade, at-risk classroom... full-time. I was burnt out, and my students were lost not only in the system but also in life. I knew I could do more, and dogs were always the answer. So, I made it happen. I was the first teacher in Clark County, Nevada, to bring a dog into a classroom full-time.

One thing led to another, and before I knew it, I was training and breeding facility dogs and service dogs. I became an AKC Canine Good Citizen Evaluator and left teaching for good. It was not an easy decision, and I returned a few times before officially resigning to follow my dream. Who would leave the security of a teaching career to become a full-time breeder? It felt risky and dumb at the time. But I believed in it like nothing else and knew I could change many lives this way. I saw what one 10-pound dog did for a classroom. I saw a need. I found my calling.

I grew quickly, faster than I could have ever imagined. We moved to a small town outside of Las Vegas where my growth could be legal and the necessary space for expansion was possible. I found valuable breeding resources far and few between. I learned as much as I could as I went. Litter after litter, I improved. I read as much as possible when new things came across my path. But ultimately, I used my intuition and trusted myself. I developed my own handling exercises, puppy curriculum, and temperament testing, which helped me honor each puppy's purpose and match them with the correct family.

I saw how so many other people were just like me. They needed a dog as much as I did. The more dogs I placed, the more stories I heard of how each one had helped their humans and saved them when they did not even know they needed to be saved. I drowned myself in my work. It was much easier to help others than to help myself. It became my coping mechanism. What I did not see coming was how my dogs, my puppies, and my clients were saving me. With each dog I placed into someone's arms, a bit of me healed, too.

I love my puppies deeply, to my core. They are safe to love, and they bring me such peace. The quiet beats of their heart thump against my hand, the smell of puppy breath on my face, and I close my eyes, feeling nothing but love. When I let them go and saw tears well up in the eyes of their new human, I realized they needed them just as much as I did. I saw how that puppy brought them hope, safety, and unconditional love. It is a beautiful thing to witness. Over time, clients opened up to me: They lost a child. Their spouse cheated. They have PTSD. They survived a mass shooting. They lost their sibling to addiction. Their mother to cancer. They were sexually abused as a child. Their anxiety is controlling their life. Their depression is ruining their life. Their hearts are broken. Their sadness is heavy. They were lost.

I was meeting the most amazing people and hearing the most incredible stories. Although heartbreaking, I also saw that their perseverance and grit to survive were strong. I saw broken people that were doing extraordinary things. They were training their puppy to be a therapy dog to work with people in hospice care. Veterans were training their dogs to help other veterans. A victim of sexual abuse as a child was now training her dog to work with courthouses when other child victims had to testify. Domestic abuse victims were training their dogs to help those in safe houses. People were turning their pain into power. They were using the power of a dog to bring comfort, hope, and even some joy. People were giving back.

People told me what they needed the dog to do, and I went to work. Raising them with my proprietary service dog curriculum and then performing a puppy evaluation, which has evolved several times over the last twelve years. By targeting the puppies with the aptitude for such work, I set both the puppy and the client up for success. As a dog's purpose unfolds, a person's heart heals.

Intertwined. One.
What a beautiful thing to witness.

I never expected that with every dog I placed into someone's heart and home, I'd begin to heal too. My faith in humanity was being restored.

I knew what I had to do. There was a great need for breeders, dogs, and clients to work together. Really work together. I had witnessed miracles right before my eyes over and over. I had become a tiny part of their story, and my dogs had become a much larger one. I was the avenue between dog and human to facilitate hope and healing. I needed to help people, and there was only one way I knew how: to provide dogs that healed hearts and saved lives. I needed to be their voice. It was time.

I cleaned up my "contacts list" in my life, so to speak, both professionally and personally. The people I needed would support my journey. Boundaries were set, and I was no longer willing to tolerate those who did not align with my goals and mission. I had big dreams, but I knew those dreams would also put me at risk for criticism. I am sensitive. I do care what people think. I knew I needed people around me to keep me moving forward, even when I was fighting self-doubt and wanted to throw in the towel. I also needed people who believed in a dog's power as much as I did.

I wanted to start giving away puppies to those that needed them most -for service dog work, therapy dog work, facility dog work, an ESA, or just a person who needed a special dog. An empowered, balanced, and happy companion. I took applications and started giving away dogs. Some untrained and some fully trained. Word spread fast, and before I knew it, local news stations and National News Stations contacted me, wanting a chance to feature a giveaway. I was also donating dogs left and right for our local community events, anything we could do to pay it forward.

I have been on the local news several times and Good Morning America three times. Our curriculum at 4E Kennels and the quality of puppies were being nationally recognized. I was producing countless working dogs. Dogs for classrooms, dentist offices, addiction centers, funeral homes, a women's prison, court houses, diabetic alert dogs, mobility assist dogs, autism support dogs, PTSD, ESA's, etc.

I would have done anything to have had a dog at the funeral home when I sat there making such awful decisions, like what box my brother would be cremated in. You see, my mother suffered a massive stroke an hour after finding my brother in his bed. When I arrived at their house and saw an ambulance, I immediately thought, I knew my brother would not leave me.

How naïve.

My mother was being put into the ambulance. Completely incoherent. Fear and panic were written across her face. I looked at my dad, and in three seconds, we decided he would go, and I would stay. I had no choice. I had to enter the house, climb the stairs, and walk into his room. Alone.

Nothing can prepare you for that. Nothing.

And then I had to plan the funeral and hope my mother could attend. My world was falling apart.

So yes, dogs entering the workforce is a necessity. It is about time we let dogs take over.

People want to know what I am doing that is so different? How come so many of my dogs are doing such incredible things? How am I raising so many puppies that are becoming working dogs? I have incredible clients; my dogs are working and accomplishing such amazing things with them. We share a vision and belief, and that is vital. I have a job, one that is not taken lightly. It comes with a hefty weight. Breed healthy dogs. Raise empowered puppies on a curriculum that works. Evaluate puppies correctly. Get people the dog they need. Get dogs the human they deserve.

I discovered something so many were missing. How you handle and manage a puppy during the first eight weeks is about so much more than just "exposing" them to new things. From how they need to be held the first two weeks to how you handle fear as they grow, these things are essential in producing the best.

Empower. Not enable.

Lastly, how the heck do you truly evaluate a pup? The truth is the ability and knowledge of breeders to accurately evaluate a puppy is lacking in so many programs. So, I started a breeder mentorship program, teaching breeders worldwide to raise and evaluate these little heart healers too.

With my big dreams to change breeding from bad to badass and bridge the gap between breeder and client, I can now bring you along on this journey. What I have learned from producing hundreds of working dogs. What I know about puppy development, what puppies need, and when and how many people get it wrong. Good owners. Best intentions. We just don't know better.

Until we do.

Come with me as I share with you how we raise all our working dogs and for the first time, give you a training plan.

Come with me on this journey as we truly understand what our canines need to be fulfilled and happy.

Come with me as I show you how incredible your relationship can be when you live in the same symbiotic place where trust and respect are the foundation and love is abundant.

Table of Contents

Chapter 1
Do I Really Want a Puppy?

When we bring a new puppy home, a range of emotions can wash over us, from excitement to even buyer's remorse. It's a phenomenon known as postpartum puppy buying, and it's a very real experience. I've witnessed numerous clients panic after acquiring a puppy, feeling overwhelmed to the point of seeking solace in the bathroom. Unfortunately, some even end up returning the puppy. This entire situation could have been avoided if we addressed it openly. The truth is we are often ill-prepared for the responsibilities that come with owning a puppy, especially if we haven't before. After all, how could we possibly know? That's why I'm here now—to equip you with the necessary knowledge and understanding. You're not alone in this. It's natural to question your decision and feel utterly overwhelmed. You might even realize that owning a puppy isn't what you truly want, and that's ok too. Unfortunately, social media has turned puppy ownership into a fashion statement, a glamorous event worthy of Pinterest and Instagram. This trend poses a problem because the reality of puppyhood can be challenging. How much you already have on your plate also becomes a significant factor. The truth is, raising a puppy requires a considerable amount of time, patience, and energy. So, ask yourself if you are truly ready for the commitment needed to raise a puppy?

Ah, the joys of puppy ownership. Let's talk about the glamorous side, shall we? Picture this: puppies unleashing a catastrophic explosion of diarrhea on your carpet. Not just once, mind you, but multiple times. They'll even manage to get it all over their kennel, with their wagging tails transforming your walls into an abstract artwork (that's why I'm all for plastic kennels, by the way).

But wait, there's more! Puppies also have a talent for vomiting. And boy, do they have eclectic taste. Legos, grass, their own food, a random sock—oh, and a rock? Seriously, a rock? Hopefully, it all came up and saved you from a frantic visit to the vet and a costly bill.

Now, let's dive into the world of potty training. The absolute pinnacle of joy! Can you sense my sarcasm? Even as a breeder, trainer, and self-proclaimed dog lover, I confess that potty training is on my list of least favorite things. And if we're being honest here, barking isn't far behind. The faster I can conquer both of these challenges, the happier I am. And a happy owner equals a happy dog or maybe it should be happy dog, happy life.

Next up, kennel training. This one has the power to test relationships and shatter souls. Sleepless nights? You bet! Puppies can scream as if their very existence is on the line, leaving us questioning our moral compass for confining them in a "cage" and enduring their ear-piercing cries. But they say it's good for them, right? And deep down, we know it is.

And finally, let's not overlook the daily exercise of chasing a mischievous puppy around, repeating "no" a hundred times a day, bending over to remove countless items from their curious mouths, and desperately trying to avoid becoming a human pin cushion, all while operating on minimal sleep.

"Get a puppy," they said. "It would be fun," they said. Well, they weren't wrong. It's a special kind of chaotic, messy, and exhausting fun that may sometimes also leave you questioning your sanity.

But…. before I talk you out of it entirely, we all know the true power of a dog and puppy raising can be endearing and rewarding, and I am here to empower you and your puppy so that you are both happy and fulfilled.

If the thought of a puppy already overwhelms you, it's important to be honest with yourself. Wait until your life aligns better with the needs and time commitment a puppy requires. Raising a well-balanced, happy dog demands serious time, effort, and dedication. But of course, the rewards are absolutely worth it. Just remember, this is not a decision to be taken lightly.

Let's dive into some essential factors to consider before getting a puppy:

1. Time commitment: Puppies need a significant chunk of your time and attention. Training, socialization, and exercise are all part of the package. Make sure you have the time and energy to invest in a puppy.

2. Financial commitment: Puppies come with ongoing expenses. Regular veterinary care, food, toys, and supplies—they all add up. Ensure that your bank account can handle your puppy's needs.

3. Living situation: Take a good look at your living space. Consider the size of your home and whether you have a yard or access to outdoor areas. Some breeds may also fit better in certain living situations. Let's find the perfect match for your space.

4. Family considerations: If you have kids or other pets, thinking about how a puppy will fit into your family dynamic is crucial. Get everyone on board and ensure they're ready for the adventure.

5. Long-term commitment: Remember, puppies grow up to become adult dogs. They'll be your loyal companions for a decade or more. Are you ready for that level of commitment? Think about the long-term picture.

If you've thought it through and are still determined to add a puppy into your life, let's get down to business. Together, we'll make this the best buying and raising experience you've ever had—a once-in-a-lifetime dog kind of experience.

And hey, if you've already had that special connection with a dog before, trust me, lightning can strike twice When it happens, beautiful things unfold, and your souls become intertwined. It all starts with finding the breed that suits your needs and then finding an ethical and responsible breeder. When we honor our dogs, their breed's integrity, purpose, and voice, we forge an unbreakable connection that transcends the human realm. And let me tell you when that happens, it's freaking amazing.

Chapter 2
Buying Responsibly

Goals are always good to have. Sometimes we reach them, and other times, we resolve to try harder, do better and try again. Having goals with your new puppy is no different. Evaluating what you really want and making sure it is realistic for you and your new puppy is important. If we do not honor what the breed was bred to do -what they were actually intended to do- then we have already failed.

It's also important to research specific breeds to learn about their health issues and any breed-specific concerns. Meeting and spending time with dogs of different breeds can also help you better understand their personalities and whether they are a good fit for you.

When choosing a dog breed, it's important to consider various factors that align with your lifestyle, preferences, and requirements. Here are some key factors to consider:

1. **Size**: Determine the size of the dog that would fit well in your living situation. Large breeds may require more space and exercise, while smaller breeds may be more suitable for apartments or homes with limited space.

2. **Energy Level**: Assess your activity level and lifestyle. Some breeds are highly energetic and require ample exercise and mental stimulation, while others are more laid-back and content with moderate exercise.

3. **Temperament**: Consider the breed's typical temperament and characteristics. Some breeds are known for being friendly and outgoing, while others may be more reserved or protective. Match the breed's temperament with your own personality and lifestyle.

4. **Grooming Needs**: Different breeds have different grooming requirements. Some breeds have minimal shedding and low-maintenance coats, while others may require regular grooming, brushing and even professional grooming.

5. **Trainability**: If you're looking for a dog that is easy to train, consider breeds known for their intelligence and willingness to please. Keep in mind that all dogs require training and socialization, but some breeds may require more consistent and structured training.

6. **Allergies**: If you or someone in your household has allergies, consider breeds that produce fewer allergens (there is really no such thing as a hypoallergenic dog). These breeds typically have hair

instead of fur and may be more suitable for individuals with allergies. If one has a saliva allergy, the breed does not matter. Don't allow the dog to lick or do not have a dog.

7. **Lifespan and Health**: Research the breed's average lifespan and common health issues associated with the breed. Understanding potential health concerns can help you prepare for future medical needs and ensure the well-being of your chosen breed.

8. **Compatibility with Children or Other Pets**: If you have children or other pets, consider breeds that are good with kids or get along well with other animals. Some breeds have a natural affinity for families and may be more tolerant and patient.

9. **Purpose:** Determine the purpose for getting a dog. Are you looking for a companion, a working dog, a guard dog, or a specific task-oriented breed? Different breeds have been bred for specific purposes, and considering their original function can help guide your choice.

10. **Breed-Specific Considerations:** Research specific breed characteristics, including exercise needs, potential behavioral traits, and special care requirements. Each breed has unique qualities and traits that should align with your expectations and lifestyle.

Remember, choosing a dog breed is a personal decision, and it's essential to research and understand the breed's needs and characteristics.

What do I mean by this, more specifically? Buying a husky when you live in Las Vegas may not be the best decision for you or the dog. You are frustrated by the copious amounts of hair and the dog's insistence to take off and or dig giant holes in your beautifully landscaped yard. Well...of course! They were bred to travel hundreds of miles, pulling a sled in the world's coldest regions. Not for the heat or for confinement.

If their innate needs are not met, they will "act out" causing frustration on both your parts.

A German Shepherd that is herding your children and nipping at their hands or clothes? The long hours in a kennel while everyone is at work only exacerbates the problem. The family thinks the dog is to blame and is then rehomed.

These are just two very general examples. Can the husky be happy and feel fulfilled in Las Vegas? Sure! The owner must be aware of his needs and honor the breed. Can a family with young children have a

German Shepherd? Sure. But they honor the breed. When we honor our breed, it is far more likely the dog will stay in your home for their lifetime. And that is a great goal to have.

So, let's be brutally honest before choosing our breed. Whether it is a purebred, hybrid breed, or an unknown mix - get as much information as possible. Critical things to consider… based on the breed's integrity, can I meet those needs? Can I live in harmony with this energy, drive, and motivation caliber? Will I be frustrated with a lazy, unmotivated dog that does not like to work and learn? Am I being fair to myself, my family, and the dog? Oh, and don't forget, within each breed, temperament variables exist, and we need to explore those as well. From high energy to lower energy. From assertive to submissive. From tenderhearted to not. From human-focused to environmentally focused. From confident to not. From innately mouthy to not. To being motivated to not. So how do you find a puppy and get the dish on their specific temperament traits?

Many have told me how overwhelming finding a breeder can be. I agree. I have learned a lot from being a buyer to becoming a breeder. I was not raised in this life, nor did I seek it out. I found this path by following my passion and love for dogs. Discerning a quality breeder with social media and professional photography can be difficult. I am with you. But I can break this down to help you navigate the breeder world so that you have the tools to find an ethical and responsible breeder. I have a program for breeders called, *"Empowered Badass Breeder"* and have provided education and support to help them raise their standards, evaluate their litters for important temperament traits and to follow and track their lines so they can continue to improve the quality of their puppies.

When you start researching breeders, below lists the essential things to look for. Like most things in life, there can be some variables, so please use your best judgment and your gut! A breeder may look great "on paper" but display some red flags. Coincidentally, a breeder may only check some boxes, but you feel good talking and working with them. The problem is there are differences in opinion on what is an "ethical" breeder.

Let's say you think a small hobby breeder is ethical. They raise one litter a year in their home. Is it ideal? What if they do not health test and they keep the puppies in one room for the entire eight to twelve weeks they have them? And because they are doing it all alone, some days the puppies do not get the time and care they need? Your updates as a buyer are far and few between, and puppy evaluations are not performed. They are under-socialized and nervous when meeting new people and being placed in new situations.

Another breeder that raises their puppies in another building on the property could be viewed as unethical. But what about if they have around-the-clock staff, a thoroughly enriching curriculum, health and temperament-tested parents, daily pictures, and videos, extensive puppy evaluations are performed, and the potential family always has timely communication from the breeder? Maybe not too shabby after all.

Strip away the idea that "raised in a home" is always a good thing or that dogs raised in a "kennel" (another building on the breeder's property) is always a bad thing. I have seen both done beautifully and both done so very poorly.

When looking at breeders, let's look at these things:

1.   **Comprehensive Website and Professional Social Media:** Look for breeders with informative websites that are easy to navigate. A well-structured website typically includes informational pages such as a home page, an about us section, a litters and puppies page, parents, standards of care and health testing page, and direct contact information. A breeder's social media presence should reflect their professionalism and commitment to their breeding program.

2.   **Testimonials:** Check for testimonials from satisfied clients across various platforms, including social media, Yelp, Google, and the breeder's website. Positive feedback from previous customers can provide valuable insights into the breeder's reputation and the quality of their puppies.

3.   **Transparency:** While physical breeder visits may not always be feasible due to potential risks like disease transmission, reputable breeders make an effort to maintain transparency in their practices. They may offer alternative options such as virtual visits, providing you with opportunities to see the breeding facility, meet the parents through pictures and videos, and gain insights into the overall environment in which the puppies are raised. By offering these avenues of transparency, responsible breeders aim to build trust and ensure you clearly understand their breeding program and mission. I am so proud of my program, puppies, and facility. I love to

show them off, but I cannot be an open door to everyone wanting to visit whenever they want. New moms trust me to ensure strangers are not allowed around her and her newborn puppies. If I cannot provide that level of trust, I will endanger my newborn puppies. And I have. It breaks my heart that I have broken their trust by allowing people to tour and visit when I had moms with their newborns in the nursery too. I have lost puppies because of it. Moms jump up to bark to "protect" (as they should) their puppies and accidentally steps on one. Or a mom is quietly protecting her puppies and lays on one. I am sorry, but until you have dealt with this loss firsthand, do not automatically assume a breeder is bad because they don't give you full access whenever you want. Can you see pictures of the parents? Can you follow the journey of your litter through lots of pictures and videos? My clients know where the puppies are raised. What the whelping box looks like, what mom looks like, what our curriculum areas look like, etc.

4. **Health Testing:** What health testing should be done for the breed of your choice? Do they suffer from bad hips? Hearts? Eye issues? Know your breed and what health testing is prudent. Please understand there are many things breeders can test for and avoid in their lines, but there are also things we cannot test for. We cannot cure cancer (believe me, I wish we could) and cannot control autoimmune disorders and other health issues. Please do not expect us breeders to do more than what has been done with humans. It is vital that breeders are health testing what is possible, tracking their lines, and removing dogs producing pups with issues. This commitment to the well-being of their canines ensures a healthier lineage and contributes to the vitality of future puppies.

5. **Care of the Dam (mom) and Sire (dad):** Assess the breeder's commitment to the well-being of the breeding dogs. This includes providing high-quality nutrition, appropriate housing, regular exercise (both physical and mental), routine veterinary care, clean living conditions, and proper grooming.

6. **Socialization and Care:** Examine how the breeder prioritizes the socialization and care of their puppies. A reputable breeder will provide a nurturing environment, exposing the puppies to stimuli that align with their developmental benchmarks. They also ensure puppies' needs are met in order, they have been empowered to believe in their abilities, and their emotional responses are guided through curriculum, giving them a safe place to learn and grow.

7. **Temperament Testing / Puppy Evaluations:** Are you provided with puppy evaluations? This is huge too. It would be best if you were allowed to have as much knowledge of a puppy you will be bringing into your life and home. Giving puppies a voice in their placement is a win-win for you and the puppy. How do you know if you can meet their needs if you don't know things like confidence level, energy, or their assertiveness level? This process ensures that the temperament of the chosen puppy aligns with your expectations and lifestyle. The puppy evaluation I devised is the Empowered Badass Breeder Puppy Aptitude Test, aka the BAB Puppy Evaluation. It focuses on necessary traits giving you knowledge on energy level, assertiveness, confidence, motivation, and human focus, to name a few.

8. **Return Policy:** Can you return the puppy at any time in their life if needed? This is non-negotiable. If we genuinely want to reduce rescue and shelter numbers, we must buy from responsible and ethical breeders that stand behind every dog they produce. Good breeders are not the issue. The issue is buyers buying from breeders who will not allow any of their puppies to be returned. This should be in their contract and one of your FIRST questions you ask. Responsible and ethical breeders stand behind every dog they produce, and having a return policy in their contract demonstrates their commitment to not only the well-being of their puppies but the responsibility to ensure none of their dogs end up in a shelter or rescue. Clearly dogs are rehomed. That is a reality. And I would prefer we normalize rehoming a dog if it is truly what is best for the dog. A dog should not have to suffer in a home where their needs are not being met because we are afraid of the stigma and backlash of rehoming. Do what is best for the dog. Period. Do better and find a home that can and will meet their needs.

9. **Environment:** It is essential to avoid making assumptions solely based on the location where the puppies are raised. While home-raised litters can offer a familiar setting, well-run kennels may also provide enriching experiences with around-the-clock staff and care. Focus instead on the breeder's commitment to maintaining a clean and stimulating environment for the puppies.

10. **Communication and Connection:** Do you connect with the breeder? Do you value their mission and focus in their breeding program? They should have a purpose beyond just producing puppies, such as improving the breed, preserving specific traits, or working toward a specific

goal (e.g., service dogs, working dogs, or competitive sports). Why are they breeding? What is their passion behind it? Do you trust them and their program and feel safe purchasing from them? Effective and timely communication with the breeder is crucial throughout the process. Look for breeders who offer regular updates, including photographs and videos that allow you to monitor the growth and development of your prospective companion.

By carefully considering these factors and asking relevant questions, you can make a well-informed decision when choosing a breeder. It's essential to support responsible and ethical breeders to reduce the number of dogs ending up in rescues and shelters.

It is also important to recognize that the term "ethical" breeder may not have a universal definition (unfortunately). Assess each breeder based on their practices, principles, and your personal comfort level. Trust your judgment and intuition when making this significant decision.

Value well-bred dogs.

Value puppies raised on a curriculum.

Value the breeder giving the puppy a voice in their placement through evaluations.

Trust the breeder behind the puppy.

Chapter 3
Embracing Our Differences

As the world becomes more aware of the power of a dog, things are getting a bit more complicated. I spend time EVERY day helping clients or prospective clients figure out what they really need and want. There is a great deal of need for more education in this area. And you know me, I love to educate! Let's review the differences in the types of working dogs to ensure you can talk to breeders using the correct vocabulary. It will help significantly not only for your benefit (time, money, and energy) but for your potential puppy as well. We must stop assuming all dogs are the same and *that all dogs* can do everything **we want** to train them to do.

If I asked you to get on a football field to play, many of you cannot. The same would be true if you were asked to get in front of 5,000 people and perform or walk into an operating room and perform life-saving cardiac surgery! Now can we grow and evolve as people and learn new skills? Absolutely! But we can't acquire a new personality or become "talented" at specific skills just because we want to. Some talent is just raw (genetic makeup at play here too) and some by hours and hours of practice. Despite the reasons for what made us who we are, we are unique.

We are worthy.

We are special.

We each have our own story and journey.

We each have our challenges and shortcomings.

We each have a purpose.

And so do our dogs.

Many dogs suffer from anxiety, overarousal, and fear. So many of our dogs are bombarded with our anxiety, our depression, and our inability to truly meet their needs…as a DOG. I am not saying that to discount them. In fact, the opposite. We do them such an injustice by humanizing them. We show them they cannot believe in themselves by "rescuing" them from problem-solving, working through uncertainty, or by mismanaging their fear. We are making them weak.

We are losing the innate power of a dog.

And we are unknowingly, many times at the root of the cause.

We can do better. We have to do better. It starts with honoring our dogs. Truly and fully. It starts with empowering and not enabling them. Even if you "rescued" them, I put that in quotes because when we attach that label to them for the rest of their lives, we are already doing them a disservice. We are already labeling them. We are already sentencing them to a life of feeling sorry for them for their past. We end up pitying them.

And no one wants to be pitied, including a dog.

The beautiful thing is that dogs do not let their past define them. They do not let a missing limb, or being blind, reduce their joy or ability to live in the moment. We do that to them because we feel sorry for them. And our feelings become theirs because they mirror us. We have created a reality for them that is skewed and unhealthy. That reality of having a human that feels pity and sorrow in association with them continues to create fearful unbalanced dogs that do not believe in their abilities. They wonder what is wrong with them when you feel pity and sorrow in association to them.

It starts with giving our puppies a voice in their placement. When we honor them for who they are, we can give them what they need and deserve.

Imagine someone advocating for you. A person who understands what you need to thrive, be happy, and feel safe. Someone who understood your strengths and weaknesses and works tirelessly to ensure you succeed. Sometimes in life, we find that person. They do not complete us; they support us to be our best through our ups and downs and self-discoveries. They are with us as we venture down new paths and encounter new journeys. They stand behind us, next to us, and sometimes in front of us when we need it most. We have a cheerleader when we need one. Someone to pick us up when we fail and someone to love us despite our shortcomings.

Our dogs need the same, with a few exceptions. They need a firm and fair leader. They need rules, boundaries, and limitations. They need clear expectations and a consistent human with proper follow-through. This is what makes them feel safe.

On some level, all our dogs are our emotional support animals. They provide comfort and companionship that we yearn for and quite frankly, need. However, there are titles we give dogs based on their trained purpose and function. Some dogs work on farms to herd cattle or protect livestock. Some dogs work with law enforcement and the military to sniff out bombs or to protect their handlers.

We also have levels of trained dogs that work for us. One is called an ESA (emotional support animal). They have no special training or certification. They are a pet that many use to help them through depression, anxiety, or other psychiatric disabilities. They do not have rights under the ADA (Americans with Disabilities Act). They do not have legal access to public places like a service dog. They used to be allowed on airplanes, but that has changed, and those rights have been revoked. Why? Because so many abused the countless loopholes. Their rights have changed several times, and I assume they will continue to do so, so the best thing to do research about them before proceeding.

A therapy dog is a dog that is a pet and undergoes specific training to work for an organization to provide support for *others*. There are large organizations where you can get your dog certified and volunteer for them. They typically have access at hospitals, schools, long-term care facilities, and maybe even options of comfort like hospice. You must pass their specific training regulations which generally includes the AKC Canine Good Citizen Test. Because they insure you, you follow their rules and regulations. You dress your dog in their vest and work specific times and places with their approval.

Facility Dogs are becoming so popular, and this excites me so much! Specific professional locations decide to have a mascot (for lack of a better term). That location decides what level of training, who pays for the dog and training, who legally owns the dog, who will insure the dog, and who cares for the dog day in and day out. The dog works for that specific location. They go to work with the handler and go back home again. Typically, a dog cannot work 40 hours a week. There are many considerations in deciding how many hours a dog should "work" a week. We look at things like the level of unpredictability, how many breaks they get, how much they are on a leash having to perform a trained command or specific task, how much human pressure is placed on them, etc. Often, I see that dogs are working too many hours, which leads to burnout (regression in training, growling at people, and avoidance are a few examples). We must make sure they get ample breaks and time to just be a dog.

Some dogs that have been placed are at schools (in all capacities - from a specific classroom, the counseling office to the principal), a funeral home, a dentist's office, a victims advocate office, a physical therapy office, counseling offices, preschools, ABA therapy centers, doctors' offices, addiction centers, prisons, jails, group homes for youth at risk, Ronald McDonald Homes, cancer treatment centers, corporate offices, news stations, and courthouses to name a few. It is overwhelming how much one dog can change an entire environment to have the most significant impact on supporting those who need it most. The real power of a dog is being realized to the fullest and is becoming more accepted in the workforce.

Service Dogs are trained with specific tasks to work for one person to help them mitigate a disability. They not only have to learn their trained tasks but also have advanced obedience and public access training. They have to be able to manage unpredictable situations that occur in public settings. They are held to a higher standard. They must be. Their handler relies on them to perform those specific trained tasks. That could be catching their high or low blood sugar for a type 1 diabetic, providing balance support, or maybe even being their eyes. Regardless of what they were trained to do, the public must not distract them. It is not that the dog is not friendly or would love someone's attention (who doesn't), but when you distract by petting, whistling, or calling to them, you are demanding their attention. And when they are focused on you, guess what? They are not paying attention to their handler. They need to be focused on their handler, who relies on them and needs them—a dog who could potentially save their life. A dog needs to know when they see other people not to seek attention from them. So please ignore service dogs (a dog in public, typically vested). I promise you. They are well-loved and cared for. They get lots of love, time, and attention. Let them work and please respect their purpose.

Chapter 4
A Voice in Their Placement

I firmly believe that magical things happen when we give our puppies a voice in their placement and ensure you get the puppy you need and want. I hope you have been given that "once in a lifetime dog" and, even better yet, a few of those.

That dog you connected with on a whole different level.

That dog that saved you.

Maybe it was the period in your life that lent you the time to spend bonding, training, and loving that dog.

Maybe it was the specific temperament of that puppy that fit with you so well.

Maybe it was just that perfect storm.

Or maybe it was a combination of all these things?

If we target the breed and temperament and find the "type" of puppy that meshes with you, the placement will be far more successful. We can keep dogs in homes if both (owner and breeder) work our tails off to make the best possible decisions. We can reduce shelter numbers. We can reduce rescue numbers. We can save lives. Buying responsibly does that.

I am thankful for those flexible and adaptable humans allowing them to take on ANY dog; however, that is not the case for many people. Considerations have to be taken into account that will influence the success of humans and canines co-existing in harmony.

Finding a breeder who can correctly articulate a puppy's voice will help immensely. You can even search for an Empowered (Badass) Breeder. They have been able to take an extensive class in evaluating puppy temperament and follow my developmental program that creates brave, eager motivated human focused puppies that enjoy working with and for their human. They believe in their own ability and have been empowered to be the best they can be. They have learned the world is safe, people are kind, and dogs are friendly.

What a beautiful start to life!

There is no perfect puppy, so knowing as much as possible about a specific puppy to ensure you feel comfortable and confident in adding them to your family is important. So please avoid the ideology that there is a PERFECT match. Just as we are imperfectly perfectly, so are they. There are "obstacle" traits and "desired" traits with any puppy you choose, considering you and your needs/lifestyle.

We can generalize some traits considered obstacle vs. desired traits, but please understand that an 8-week-old puppy is still a PUPPY. Life experiences with you can and will deter and or provide proper development. Let's be honest. It will be both. We cannot put our puppy in a bubble and control outside influences. But what we can do is control how we help them through fear and insecurities. Whether or not we empower them or enable them. Whether we hold high expectations. Whether we reward over excitement and frenzied thinking.

Or will we raise, and reward balanced? Neutrality? Bravery? That will make a world of difference.

Considerations must be addressed if you have young children (typically ten years or younger) in your home. It is not that we think young children are mean or that you can't manage a young child and a puppy. It is that we know that if we don't honor the puppy, we are only failing you both.

Some puppies do not have the nerve strength or touch tolerance to live with younger children. Some puppies are far too assertive (bossy) to live with children. We need a middle-of-the-road, go-with-the-flow puppy that is up to being pushed in a stroller one minute and then attending a chaotic at home birthday party the next. Little hands may not always hold appropriately, but the puppy happily adapts and loves his people regardless.

In a home with young children, we must remember that our puppies also need "protection" from children. Puppies require a great deal of sleep and quiet time. They left their breeder's home where there was structure, safety, and humans who spoke their language. They go from one set of hands to another in seconds and their whole world changes immediately. Sometimes into a home of inappropriate handling and typically *too* much handling. They get overtired and crabby, which can lead to a puppy that feels like they must stand up for himself since the adult is not, which can present with growling, biting, and overall naughtiness. They are trying to tell you that while they adore their new small human siblings, they must also be respected and honored.

Let's break down puppy raising so that it makes sense and aligns with how a dog thinks and communicates while also making it feasible for you to raise a happy, well-balanced dog that does not suffer from anxiety, fear, neuroticism, or aggression.

You don't need to be a professional dog trainer, but you need to understand what a dog needs to thrive and how our actions can negatively or positively impact their growth and development.

Chapter 5
Parvo Concerns

Let's tackle an owner's worst nightmare in the bacteria world: the parvovirus. "Canine parvovirus (CPV) is a highly contagious viral disease of dogs that commonly causes acute gastrointestinal illness in puppies. The disease most often strikes in pups between six and 20 weeks old, but older animals are sometimes also affected." (https://www.vet.cornell.edu/departments-centers-and-institutes/baker-institute/our-research/canine-parvovirus)

Too often, I see new owners picking up their puppies and taking them straight to the pet store. Getting pet supplies for your new bundle of joy is exciting and fun! Yes, but no. You are stacking too much stress on your new puppy, plus exposing them to a place where parvo could be a genuine risk. After all, everyone is doing the same thing with their brand-new puppy, never knowing at that time if the puppy has parvo or not.

Instead, it would help if you kept your puppy home during the adjustment period, only leaving for a veterinarian appointment to get your puppy any necessary vaccines/deworming/microchip, etc., plus get their vaccine schedule and appointments lined up. Breeders should be handing off a puppy that has been vaccinated (they still need more as they age), dewormed (they may need to be dewormed again in 2-3 weeks), microchipped, and seen by a vet before placement to receive the all clear to go home. Setting up a "wellness" exam with your veterinarian to establish your puppy is important. You also want to make sure your vet feels you received a healthy puppy. We ask our buyers to see a veterinarian within three days to set up their next visit for their vaccines. Flea and tick medication and other area needed medications should also be discussed.

If you take home a puppy last minute and are not prepared, please take the puppy home, and then go to the pet store. Remember now that you have a puppy that is likely susceptible to parvovirus (which can be deadly), so remove shoes before returning to the home or sanitize them. The parvovirus is spread by feces and is quite virulent and hardy. It can live in an environment where a puppy has defecated. It then can be transferred to shoes, clothes, and hands with or without evidence of feces seen by the naked eye.

You can clean with bleach or heat to do your best to kill the virus. There is also disinfectants specifically to kill the parvovirus. Your veterinarian uses these types of cleaners in their clinics, and breeders use them in their kennel to help reduce the chance of the parvovirus infection. No breeder is immune from the parvovirus striking their kennel unless they and their dogs/puppies live entirely isolated, and no one comes and goes. That is neither realistic nor developmentally conducive for a puppy. So, the trick is to lead with a healthy balance of reducing the chance of infection in and outside their kennel.

One way to do that for a breeder is to have a shoe and hand cleansing protocol and limit visitors. I know you want to tour their property, meet the parents, and see the litter. Still, please understand that if you are not allowed to enter their property, there are reasons why, like the greater chance of parvo (and other viruses and bacteria) being brought in. That is terrifying for a breeder. If you trust your breeder and have vetted them properly (they have met the standards of health testing, care, living arrangements, and puppy raising) please respect their need to keep their kennel as "clean" as possible. I hope though, you have been given access to where the puppies are being raised, their curriculum activities, their parents, etc. via pictures and video.

Breeders can be open and transparent without having people coming in and out. When our clients enter the property to select and take home their puppy, they walk through two "foot baths" upon entering. One is bleach and the other a broad-spectrum disinfectant. And then, they put sterile booties over their shoes. We then lead them to a sink where they wash their hands with parvosol and antibacterial soap. Is this system foolproof? Unfortunately, not. But we do our best to balance the line between being accessible (we have nothing to hide) and reducing our chances of inadvertently having parvo or other nasty things brought in that can and will take out an entire litter. No breeder wants to send that email to clients.

As an owner, you must reduce the chance of introducing the parvovirus to your puppy's gastrointestinal system via the mouth (licking). They could step in the grass, lick their paw, and boom. Three to five days later, they exhibit the symptoms and test positive. Some puppies suffer very little and are on the mend quickly, and others perish. The parvovirus is much like the human flu, with no cure, leaving us with supportive care being our only option. It dehydrates a puppy due to vomiting and diarrhea. The action plan is to try to stop/manage the vomiting and diarrhea while keeping the puppy hydrated and electrolytes balanced as much as possible via intravenous fluids. Suppose your puppy is severe and the option is available, you can opt to have a plasma transfusion given in hopes of some parvo antibodies are introduced to restore some white blood cells and albumin (a liver protein to boost blood volume).

If any puppy stops eating, is lethargic, and has vomiting or diarrhea, a vet trip immediately is recommended. A puppy that does not eat is always a concern. Other things could be going on, but a veterinarian will almost always run a parvovirus test first to rule that out.

How can we best avoid the parvovirus while raising a well-balanced dog? We know there are behavioral consequences when we do not properly socialize and expose our dogs to new situations, places, and people. The first sixteen weeks of a puppy's life if the most crucial developmentally. So, we ask, what are the chances in "this area" that the parvovirus could lurk? When traveling home from picking up my puppy or during exposure activities when my puppy is not fully vaccinated, I constantly ask, "What are the chances a dog has defecated here?" If the chances seem low, we proceed with a potty break on the ground. I am talking about some random place off the side of the road. Not a rest stop. Not a grassy area. Watch for any scat on the ground as well. The canine parvovirus is not as specific as some of the other parvoviruses. It can affect most dog family members, like wolves, foxes, coyotes, etc. So please proceed with caution in areas where they might reside.

Now that I have thoroughly scared you, here are a few things I suggest; however, use them at your own risk. Similar to all aspects of life, there are inherent risks associated with making decisions. Striving to navigate the path forward with a keen focus on the well-being of your puppy's mental and physical development while ensuring their safety remains a constant challenge.

1. Avoid any grassy area. The parvovirus can happily live in the grass for up to a year.
2. Avoid any housing where parvo may have been introduced. Typically, the parvovirus can live in a house and yard for up to a year. So, if your previous puppy had it and you live in the same place, and it has been under a year, you are taking a chance. Big time. If you have surfaces you can clean with heat and or bleach properly; you might be ok. If you have moved into a new place within a year, my first question is, "Is there grass?" or do you know if the previous family had a puppy? That would be my biggest concern.
3. All four off the floor! You can safely see the world even if paws are not on the ground. Remember, your shoes must be removed at the door or sanitized. To keep all four paws off the ground, you can push them in a stroller or carry them in a pack.
4. I need to find out where your hands have been! Until my puppy is fully vaccinated, stranger danger is real. I am putting my puppy at risk by letting someone pet my puppy or by letting my puppy lick

someone else. So, if you have a hand that reaches for them, slap it. No! Just kidding (kind of). I always say, "I am sorry, we cannot visit because we are not fully vaccinated yet. If I feel inclined, I will ask if they have had any contact with a puppy in the last 2-3 days. If not, I may let them pet my puppy, if they are in a calm state of mind and not exhibiting any stress signals.

5. Avoid other unknown dogs where your puppy naturally sniffs their bum. If you know the owners and feel they are "safe," take them to their house for socialization or invite them over. I ensure the established dog has not gone to the groomer, a veterinarian, or a dog park within the last 72 hours.

6. Walk on the sidewalk or edge of the sidewalk (even on the side of the road) in a quiet cul de sac. The chance of a dog pooping there is slim. But the grassy knolls? Higher chance. You can also put shoes on your puppy for walks (you will have to expose them to your puppy slowly in the house first), remove them, and wipe them down when you get home. You can also just wipe their paws off with a baby wipe (it doesn't kill parvo, though, but better to try to wipe it off than not try at all). Choosing places for them to walk where the chance of infection is low, plus adding extra steps like sanitizing paws/shoes, is good. Please do not use anything harsh on their paws that would cause issues on the pad of the paw itself or from them ingesting a toxin by licking on their paw later.

Chapter 6
Your First 3-5 Days at Home

One of the greatest mistakes you can make after taking home your new puppy is wanting to show them off to everyone. And take them everywhere. But it is just way too much. They haven't even had the opportunity to bond with you and learn that *you* can be trusted yet. They do not know that you will catch their stress signals and not ask them to do anything they are not ready to do. They don't know where they are sleeping yet. Where they are supposed to potty at and all the general ins and outs of their new home. Everything in their life has changed. They have left their mama, their littermates, and their first humans. Everything is new to them. Trust me. This is enough exposure for them for now. Your more confident puppies typically only need three days to adjust and settle in. Your more sensitive puppies may need five days.

Do you have an established dog at home? Firstly, I hope you do not bring home a young and impressionable puppy to a dog at home that is fearful, overly anxious or has other behavioral issues. A young puppy will look to the established dog for feedback first. Are they the mentor you want for your puppy despite how much you love them? It is also important to note that even if your established dog is squared away and you are happy with their behavior and training, you will also need to do things separately. Take walks with just the puppy. Or just the established dog. I would not kennel them together either. You want to ensure your puppy does not develop an unhealthy relationship with the established dog. Feeling bad for the puppy is also unnecessary if you have them sleep in the kennel, but the established dog doesn't anymore. Or the established dog is allowed on the bed, but the puppy is not yet. If your established dog has EARNED those privileges, nothing should change for them. Your puppy must earn all of those rights just as your established dog did.

So how do you introduce a puppy to your established dog? First, please do not ask the breeder to take your dog to meet the puppy. That is, honestly, unfair. And here is why.

First, allowing another dog on the property could be deadly for a breeder. You could accidentally bring in something that would wipe out an entire unvaccinated litter. Or what if your dog did attack a puppy? My moms also 100% trust me, and if I allowed that, I would be breaking their trust. Secondly, what are you worried about if you have a well-behaved dog that respects you? Surely, you are not bringing in a puppy with an aggressive dog at home? It is absolutely normal if your established dog does not immediately like your puppy. But if you have a healthy bond, your established dog will not only take in the young puppy, but they will help you raise the puppy as well. Watching their bond grow is fun and rewarding. I have had so many clients come back for a second puppy. Who were they buying the new puppy for? Their established dog! I love that people recognize that dogs do love to live together. The caveat is if your established dog is geriatric and or has medical conditions. It will be crucial for you to have separate spaces for both. A young healthy puppy wants to play with (torment) their elders. And they will happily pester the heck out of them.

Have them meet outside in your backyard. If your adult dog might be overly excited, have them on a leash. If your adult dog can be in a down stay, do that. Have the meeting no-nonsense and straightforward. Here is our new family member. Period. Just be ready to manage excitement or initial disdain. Do not push anything and let things happen organically. I love the separate puppy living space for our established dogs too. It gives them a break and a sense of safety as well.

So how can you help your puppy adjust to their new home in an empowering way?

Set up a schedule. Prepare a safe space for them to live in (the smaller the area, the quicker they will potty train). All too often potty-training issues are because we make the mistake of giving a puppy the whole house. And those little stinkers are more than happy to potty in one area, play in another and sleep in a third place. They are delighted when there is carpet in the house. It is magical stuff. First, it has a lot of different scents, making it a prime place to add more. Secondly, their pee disappears, and they don't have to step in it.

I urge you to remove the availability of carpet initially by using fencing or picking it up. One of the best investments is buying temporary fencing (baby gates or the like) and reducing the space the puppy has available to them. To make it even better, back the fencing up to the back door (or wherever you want them to exit to their potty space) and begin the foundation of where they sleep (inside) and where they potty (outside). This short-term solution will give you max benefits in potty training a puppy. It is also a safe practice to contain and monitor a puppy, especially if you have children and a large house.

The best way to lay a solid foundation is through prevention and not allowing puppies to get into mischief and trying to fix things. I would much prefer prevention and distraction over trying to correct/fix. And who else thrives on firmness and kindness? Consistency and structure?

That's right, your puppy.

To avoid the possibility of separation anxiety (some breeds and temperaments area more prone to this troublesome behavior) please ensure you do leave the puppy alone. I have had clients initially take a few weeks off of work to be with the puppy 24/7. While having the uninterrupted time to help a puppy transition can be helpful, by not leaving their side can cause separation anxiety. So, day 2, put the puppy in the kennel (no emotions or feeling bad – be brave) and leave. When you come home, no emotion and let the puppy out to potty. No high-pitched talking. No petting. No excitement. I know it is hard but look at it from the puppy's point of view. You put them in the kennel and feel badly about it (they feel your emotions) and wonder why you have a negative association to the kennel and then leave them in it. Then you leave. When you come home? You are excited, baby talk, rush to them. Pet them. On and on. Soooo confusing! Now there is a lot of excitement surrounding the kennel? What gives?

Be matter of fact. Be fair. Be consistent. Have a safe and calm presence. They will trust that. They will trust that you leave. You will come back. They will live.

Leaving a high value item / brain game (raw bone, Kong with a tiny bit of peanut butter, etc.) in the kennel when you leave also makes the kennel a more inviting experience. Be consistent. If you let a puppy out of the kennel when crying, you have taught them that it works. They just need to cry long enough and loud enough, and you cave. So, don't. Some puppies take longer to realize what is expected of them then others.

One of the biggest issues with a new puppy is poop. Diarrhea to be more specific. We have a few simple but effective rules to follow to help the transition succeed and limit the opportunity for diarrhea to ensue. And believe me, if you have never had a puppy with diarrhea, I would like to keep it that way.

I have found after years of selling puppies, collecting data, and tweaking the go-home protocol, is too much stress and too much change in diet (change of food and treats) is a huge catalyst to the cause of diarrhea and GI upset. We have seen such great success with this go-home protocol to help keep the odds of digestive upset to a slim chance. I know it doesn't make sense that dogs eat dead things, their poop, and whatever awful thing we can think of, but for crying out loud, switching their food or giving them a new treat and gasp… everything goes to shit.

Literally.

It is not fair. I know. But it is the reality.

• No treats. Please use their kibble as treats (before feeding) for as long as possible.

• Please do not change the food they came on for at least nine weeks. Think in 9's with dog food. Do not switch for nine weeks but if you want to or need to, do it over nine days.

First 3 Days	Next 3 Days	Last 3 Days
75% breeder food and 25% new food	50% of each food	25% breeder food and 75% new food

While I am not a dog food snob and there is so much information about dog food and nutrition, I know that there is no such thing as one great food for all dogs. I will say that if your dog is thriving on a particular food and is healthy with solid poop, I would think carefully about messing with a food change.

Here are some other important guidelines to follow to help your puppy adjust and limit GI upset!

• Do not wake a sleeping puppy! Puppies need a great deal of sleep, especially during the transition into a new home. Please make sure they get good quality sleep that is not often interrupted.

• Keep things consistent. Don't allow them on the couch if they are not allowed on the couch. If they have to sleep in their kennel, start that night. Make sure all humans in the house implement and maintain the SAME rules for the puppy. It makes it confusing and stressful for a puppy and unfair if the rules are inconsistent.

• Continue using the "yes" empowerment word (Empowered Badass Breeders have started this) to remind them they are brave! Yes, they can do it! And yes, they can trust you as they explore their new home and yard.

• Do not overcorrect or use the "No" word constantly. We don't want them to think their name is "No". They will tune you out. Instead, prevent and redirect. If they are chewing on your shoes, that is a failure on your part. If they potty in the house, that is a failure on your part. If these things are happening adjust and learn and prevent it from happening again. They don't know what is allowed to chew on and what is not. They don't know the rules of where to potty or what areas of the house they are not allowed. It is all fair game unless you prevent it from happening to begin with. You cannot scold a puppy for something you allowed. I give lots of positive praise for catching a puppy doing something good! I name it and reward it! They sit and look at me. I say "sit" and reward! I would much rather be the giver than the taker.

Over-excitement in puppies can become a problem if it is not managed correctly. Puppies are naturally exuberant creatures filled with energy and excitement; however, when their excitement reaches an excessive level, it can become challenging for both the puppy and their owners to handle.

I want to mention that "puppy zoomies," Frenetic Random Activity Periods (FRAPs), describe the energetic bursts of activity and excitement seen in dogs and puppies. Zoomies refer to those moments when they exhibit sudden and uncontrolled bursts of energy, often characterized by running, spinning, and playful behavior. These episodes can occur spontaneously and typically happen when puppies feel excited, happy, or have excess energy to burn. Common activities that are followed by a zoomie episode are after bath time, training, long periods of confinement, early in the morning, or late at night. FRAPs are normal behavior and a healthy outlet for a puppy's energy. They are generally harmless if the environment is safe, and no objects or obstacles could cause injury. I suggest that during these normal but crazy times, you have your puppy release their energy outside. I also strongly suggest that children not be involved in puppy zoomies. Let the puppy safely drain their silliness outside where it is safe, and you are not rewarding or promoting any play that could be rough or out of control. Sit back, watch, and smile. Puppy zoomies are an important reminder that your puppy is healthy AND happy. And as they age, these episodes decrease, which can be disheartening.

Ok, back to overexcitement that is not zoomies and can disrupt daily routines, hinder training progress, and strain the bond between you and your puppy. It may also contribute to undesirable behaviors, such as destructive chewing, nipping, humping, barking, or ignoring commands. Addressing overexcitement is essential for fostering a well-behaved, balanced, and happy puppy.

Here are some strategies to help you through periods of unwanted overexcitement:

1. **Meeting their needs in order (more in chapter 8):** Consistent rules, boundaries, and limitations are vital in teaching a puppy self-control and impulse management. Mental and physical exercise is vital. Bored and frustrated puppies do not know what to do with all their energy. Engage puppies in puzzle toys, treat-dispensing games, obedience training, and scent work to challenge their minds and

keep them busy. Providing puppies with regular exercise and physical activity helps to channel their energy positively. Incorporate daily walks, play sessions, and interactive toys to tire them out. Love and affection should only be given when they are in a calm state of mind and only after their other needs have been met.

2. **Calm Environment:** Create a calm and predictable environment for your puppy. Avoid chaotic situations, excessive noise, or overstimulation that may increase excitement. Establish a designated quiet space where they can relax and unwind. And remember to initially keep their available space small. A kennel is a great space for a calm and "safe" space for puppies where kids are not allowed. Or help your puppy settle with a leash (more on this to come) and your calm energy. No reaching, petting, or provoking.

3. **Set Realistic Expectations:** Understand that puppies have bursts of energy and may sometimes exhibit overexcitement. Be patient and consistent with your training efforts, reinforcing calm behaviors and positive reinforcement for desired actions. Ignore behaviors (not scold or reward with petting or vocal praise/baby talk). Make a mental note to prevent or distract from the trigger next time. Some things can often be seen as "cute" when they are a puppy, but it becomes problematic as an adult dog.

4. **Socialization and Controlled Interactions:** Proper socialization with other dogs, humans, and different environments is crucial. Introduce puppies to new things slowly and in a controlled way, ensuring it's a positive experience without overwhelming them. Watch when other people or other dogs create over-excitement and manage accordingly. Redirection and prevention are ideal.

Chapter 7

10 Step Puppy Handling Exercises

Breeders can raise puppies to be compliant to touch. There is no reason why a puppy should have an aversion to being touched. They live with and among humans. Touch is not only natural; it is healthy. Wanted. Desired. However, there is touch that is not desired. There will be touch that is painful and unwanted but necessary. Grooming appointments can be uncomfortable. Every dog needs veterinarian care. Every dog will have an injury or a medical need at some point. We can't avoid or protect them from these interactions. I hate going to the dentist. Everything they do is uncomfortable for me. I wish I never had to go! But I have too, regardless of how much I dislike it. The same is for our dogs. We can't protect them from handling that will be aversive, but we can create compliant dogs that, at a minimum, tolerate handling. I have devised a 10-step handling exercise that aligns with their sensitive developmental benchmarks. It is just as important for me as a breeder to begin this exercise as it is for you to continue doing them. While we can't change a puppy on how much they enjoy different types of handling, we can create touch-compliant dogs. Not only will your veterinarian and groomer thank you, but you and your dog will benefit too.

Performing regular handling exercises with your puppy is a valuable practice that promotes their physical and emotional development and strengthens the bond between you and your puppy. While you don't have to do this exercise daily, engaging in it several times a week is important (see the 4-week training plan in the forms section at the back of the book). It's recommended that all family members participate in the 10-step handling exercise to ensure consistency and familiarity for your puppy.

Here's a step-by-step guide to the 10 step handling exercises:

1. Start by covering your puppy's eyes gently. This step helps them anticipate and trust the process of being handled.

2. Rub and gently tug on their ears. This allows you to inspect their ears for cleanliness and helps make sure they are comfortable with gentle manipulation.

3. Open their mouth and inspect their teeth and gums. Check for any signs of teething or alignment issues. This step helps familiarize your puppy with mouth handling and dental care.

4. Rub their belly in a wide circular motion. This mimics a gentle belly rub and promotes relaxation and trust.

5. Rub your hand up their back. This helps acclimate them to various levels of touch and prepares them for different types of petting they may encounter in the future, such as children or unfamiliar individuals.

6. Gently tug and twist their tail. This step assists in desensitizing them to tail handling, which is important for grooming, veterinary care, and a possible toddler grab!

7. Rub your fingers in between the pads of their paws. This action familiarizes them with touch on their paw pads and can help prepare them for future paw care.

8. Tap lightly on the tip of their nails. This helps desensitize them to the sensation of nail trimming or filing, making future nail care easier.

9. Place your hand around their collar and gently tug and slide it around. This ensures your puppy is comfortable with collar touches and prevents aversion to collar handling.

10. Touch their nose gently. This reinforces trust and teaches your puppy to accept gentle touches on their sensitive facial area.

By regularly performing these handling exercises, you not only teach your puppy compliance and reinforce trust, but you also contribute to their overall socialization and confidence. Puppies frequently handled are more likely to grow into well-adjusted, confident, and friendly adult dogs.

On top of teaching compliance to touch, here are four reasons why handling a puppy is essential:

1. **Socialization:** Handling a puppy is a crucial part of their socialization process. By handling a puppy from a young age, you can help them become accustomed to different people, environments, and situations. This can prevent fear and aggression issues later in life. Just don't overhandle and or let too many strangers handle your puppy. Watch for any stress signals (yawning, avoidance, lip smacking, panting, etc.) and then make sure you stop the handling. Your puppy is telling you they need a break.

2. **Bonding:** Handling a puppy can help you form a bond with them. Holding, petting, and massaging your puppy can help them feel safe and secure in their new home. And who doesn't love a good massage?

3. **Training:** Handling a puppy can also make it easier to train them. Getting your puppy used to being handled makes performing routine tasks such as nail trimming, grooming, and veterinary exams easier. The 10-step puppy handling exercises are genuinely life-changing for your puppy!

4. **Health:** Handling a puppy can also help you monitor their health. By holding and examining your puppy frequently, you can identify any health issues early on and seek treatment promptly. Getting your hands on them daily from head to tail, you can quickly catch any potential health issues/ concerns.

Overall, handling a puppy a lot is an essential part of their development. By providing them with plenty of positive interactions and socialization experiences, you can help them grow into confident, well-adjusted adult dogs. Assure all love and affection is done after their innate needs have been met, and you do so when they are in a calm state of mind. Otherwise, you could be inadvertently rewarding "the crazy" in a puppy and or creating anxiety. Love and affection should be given when both human and dog are centered.

Focused. Calm. Loving.

It is a truly a form of meditation - for both.

Chapter 8
Meeting Their Needs in Order

I love that dogs tell us their love language and do so very clearly. While each dog has variables for each of these needs, this is the foundation of a dog. How beautiful would life be if humans could clearly communicate their needs in a manner that makes sense and then is not impossible to be met by themselves or another? We have been given the gift of being able to understand canine psychology.

To be able to witness it.
To live in their moment.
To let them settle into our souls.

We don't slow down enough to realize how powerful their brain is. They do not live in the past. Dogs have a remarkable ability to live in the present moment and let go of past experiences. Unlike humans, who often carry emotional baggage from past traumas, dogs have a natural resilience and a unique ability to move forward without dwelling on the past.

Dogs live in the here and now, focusing on present experiences, sensations, and interactions that surround them. They are not burdened by regret, guilt, or worry about what has happened in the past. Instead, they embrace each moment with enthusiasm and an open heart.

This quality can inspire humans, reminding us to let go of past traumas and not allow them to define our present and future. Dogs teach us the power of forgiveness, resilience, and the ability to find joy in the simplest moments.

They do not dwell. Hate. Judge.

They can love entirely without judgment or bias. They can mirror our emotions without expectation. They can feel us rather than see us, which is the most powerful thing. They don't care how much we weigh, what color hair we have, if we are bald, short, broke, tall, hairy, religious, our political views, etc.

They feel us for who we are as a person.

Our heart.

Our kindness.

Our stability.

Our fairness.

Our consistency.

Our ability to lead with strength and bravery.

So, what are we letting our dogs feel from our souls? If you lead with anger, unpredictability, inconsistency, coddling, or pity, our dogs now live in an uncertain world with an unreliable human. If they have had a negative experience and it was not rewritten correctly, they will continue to live with uncertainty. They will still be loyal to us and love and comfort us, but you have not given them what they need. We are ruining our dogs. God love us. We don't mean to. We love them more than most other people for crying out loud, but we are creating anxious, fearful, and neurotic dogs. We don't know any better. We forget our dogs are more powerful than we will ever be. In a world of so much uncertainty, a world where we struggle to know where we belong. Where our worth lies. Our dogs are waiting for us to see if we are brave enough to stand in our own space.

Without fear.

So, they can have safe and consistent leadership.

Regardless of what you may be struggling with in your life, your dog needs to know that you are *almost* always there for them (no one can be 100% all the time). To meet their needs. To provide safety through proper leadership. To continue to empower them to be their best. To honor them for who they are. To respect them. To love them. But love them like they are a canine and not a human. Truly. Innately. And when that happens, the soul of a dog and a human are intertwined as one. In a way, you will never experience with a human.

If we can't meet our dog's needs, we must stop asking them to meet all of ours. That is more than fair. It must be a symbiotic relationship. One based on trust and respect. A relationship we all desire with our dog (and humans too). But the beautiful thing about your dog is that this relationship is attainable and will not falter or fail as many human relationships do.

One of the best ways to guarantee a healthy and balanced relationship is to meet your dog's needs in order. Oh... we get this so wrong, but the amazing thing is that with a few mindset changes, this will be life-changing for you and more importantly, your dog.

A dog's first innate, fundamental need, not counting food/water/shelter, is rules, boundaries, and limitations. Not affection.

I am just trying to picture your face right now! Lol!

I know, crazy, right? What the heck? Our dog innately needs structure? Consistency? Rules? Expectations?

YES!!!!

Dogs want to know what is expected of them and the consequences to be fair and consistent. They want to know where they stand. What they can get away with and what they can't. Depending on the dog's temperament, some will challenge far more than others. It would help if you matched the assertiveness level of your puppy to what you are comfortable with and capable of managing effectively. Be honest with yourself. Are you a pushover? Are you able to hold your ground? Some puppies are just "easier" in this area. A firm low growl of "no," and they got the message loud and clear. And then there are some puppies and breeds that require a higher intensity correction. We will talk about correctly communicating with a puppy later.

What are reasonable and realistic rules, limitations, and boundaries in a home? Some of that depends on what you want and need from your dog. If you allow your dog (especially a puppy) to have access to every room and every elevated surface, this need is more challenging to meet. I suggest limited space initially, with no couches, chairs, or beds. If it is something you want, please have them earn that right first by establishing the groundwork initially. It is easier to allow more and more "rights" as they earn them, rather than trying to go back and fix any foundational behavioral concerns.

Other rules and limitations look like, kennel training (this is where you sleep and you will do so quietly), potty training (this is where you will go potty), spatial limitations (you do not get to go upstairs yet), appropriate items to put your mouth on (we only chew on these toys). With a puppy, prevention and redirection is so important. We don't put teeth on people, we don't chase the cat, we keep all four paws on the ground (don't pet and praise them when they jump on you), we don't beg for food (so don't feed them from the table).

As our puppies age, these rules, boundaries, and limitations will shift and change just as they do when raising our children. But there should always be constants, and those would be: no jumping on people (unless trained by command when to do so), no leash reactivity, no bossy or incessant barking, no putting teeth on a human (unless trained to do so), no dog aggression, no taking food that is not yours, no putting items in your mouth that is not yours (unless trained to do so), no guarding any of your items, to name a few.

The second need of your dog is mental and physical stimulation. Not love and affection yet! I know you may now be shaking your head and questioning me, but these are our canine's innate needs. Not ours. So, please hear me out.

If dogs do not get physical exercise proper to their breed and energy level, they will exhibit many behavioral issues. It is really a shame when humans choose a breed that they are unwilling or uncapable of meeting their energy needs. I will go first. Hi. My name is Jeanette, and I do not have the time, energy, or desire to have a high-energy dog. That does not make me a bad dog owner or a bad person. It just means, I need to be careful about what breed and then what puppy I choose to live with. The teacher in me does far better at mental stimulation through brain games and training. I don't like taking long walks. I just don't. So, I cannot commit to owning a dog that needs miles a day. Being honest with myself and my needs is important before bringing a puppy home and just as importantly (or more), the puppy. Please research breeds (mixed or not, whatever you fancy) and buy from an empowered breeder who can evaluate energy levels within their breed/program. A high-energy dog is more likely to be taken to the shelter than a lower-energy dog. So please take this seriously and be honest with yourself and your lifestyle (other commitments, time, desires, etc.).

Dogs love to feel accomplished, just as we do. To work *for* something. To love their "work" or have the satisfaction of completing something. And that could be as simple as getting peanut butter out of a Kong or as complex as being a seeing eye dog (Guide Dog) where they have to independently problem solve without cues from their human.

Mental stimulation can be in the form of training! Whether it is obedience or trick training (things for fun like, shake, play dead, etc.). Activities that require mental and physical exercise are fantastic, like agility work, herding, and search and rescue, to name a few. And most of us will not require nor have the lifestyle ability to have that level of a working dog. A family pet can also have both needs met simultaneously. A game of fetch can also actually meet the first innate need for rules, boundaries, limitations, and mental and physical exercise. This is where we can get creative and have fun with something that seems so simple. We can level up, which will also level up your relationship with our dog. Win-win! Fetch with rules, like dropping the ball in my hand. So rather than throwing the ball and letting your dog fetch it, sniff a few bushes on the way back, and then sometimes not even giving the ball back to you, forcing you to have to grab it from their mouth, I challenge you to do something like this instead: before throwing the ball, have your dog "sit." You can raise the obedience level and have your dog wait to get the ball until you release them. This takes a great deal of time and practice so I will give you a more practical option first. Throw the ball, have your dog retrieve it, bring it back, sit, and place it in your hand. I did this with one of my retrievers (Eloise), and she got pretty dang good at it. If she missed my hand, she knew to try again! I didn't have to wrangle the ball from her mouth and was meeting her needs in order. I think my expert training was excellent, if I say so myself, and I was happy I didn't have to bend over to pick up the ball 100 times a day.

I am just keeping it real here.

The third and last innate need for dogs is ding ding ding; you got it!!! Love and affection. I have found how powerful it is to only give love and affection when they are in a calm state of mind but also after their other two needs have been met. It is more natural. It is reciprocal. It comes from a place of respect and true connection. You both can be present in the moment, and it is not diluted with excitement or stained with fear or uncertainty.

Make sure to distinguish love and affection from positive praise. I am my dog's biggest cheerleader and will dish out lots of verbal and physical praise (quick pat) for a job well done. Just like humans, we want to know we are doing good. We want reassurance. We want guidance. We want fair and consistent leadership. And if we are already a leader/boss in our life, a good one, it is done with fairness, lots of positive praise, uh, I mean positive affirmation, and rewards (bonuses, raises, trips, work meals, whatever motivates your team). A dog is no different. After they have worked hard, they want a sincere reward too. Every dog is different, but most want love and affection, a toy, or food. These three things can also motivate a dog to work/train!

Man, this relationship sounds easier and easier. You are thinking right now…wait? This seems too simple. Let me get this right. I have to meet their three needs in order and then find out their favorite reward/motivation (three to pick from), and my dog will benefit greatly?

Yes. In a nutshell. And most dogs love all three rewards, so it is figuring out which they prefer as their top choice to really benefit you both. Beautiful things happen when we interact with our dog with meaning and purpose.

At 4E Kennels and through my Empowered Badass Breeder Program, we look at how this is done from the moment our puppies are born. How our moms continue to have their needs met in order. How our relationships are created and cultivated on trust and respect and not dominance or alpha rolling. How our puppies are raised to feel safe and empowered. How they are constantly reminded that they can believe in their abilities and feel fulfilled and thrive.

But what does this look like for you too?
It is exciting to share this with you because I know how so many of my clients have benefited from making sure their puppy's needs are being met in order.

For example, you wake up in the morning and take the puppy out of the kennel (they sleep in the kennel, so that is a rule), and then they go outside to potty (rule). After that, you play fetch with them, and you ask them to drop the ball at your feet (mental and physical stimulation) and then you both go inside to eat breakfast. As you are serving their breakfast, you have them sit politely (rule and mental work) and then they get fed. After they eat, you call them over and give them some cuddles (love and affection). Depending on your schedule, you will repeat everything in order of their needs as much as possible. If you leave for work, you will put them in their kennel (rule) and leave. When you go home, you will enter without excitement and let them outside to potty (rule) and then give them the proper opportunity for physical exercise while outside (physical need). You can call them in and practice obedience or perform the "sit on the dog" exercise, tether training, or hand-feeding their dinner (more on this in Chapter 12). When they are in a calm state of mind, then you give love and affection. As puppies get older, your tighter schedule and focus on meeting their needs in order will wane because you have laid the foundation. Your puppy knows what to expect. They know the rules, boundaries, and limitations and if they forget, you remind them fairly and firmly. You have daily activities that meet their mental and physical exercise needs and provide love and affection in a calm state of mind. Your puppy will have been raised through expectation while having *their* needs met.

While feeling safe.

While understanding what is expected of them.

While being treated with respect and fairness.

While feeling like they are understood.

While feeling accomplished.

While having fun.

While being loved.

And that is a powerful thing.

For both canine and human.

Chapter 9
How We Handle Fear Matters

How we handle fear in our dogs is vital to their lifelong success of being happy and fulfilled.

Of feeling secure.

Of being balanced.

Of living life in peaceful harmony with their humans.

Unfortunately, when we react to our puppy's fear like they are a human child, we are conveying the wrong message. They are not human. We already talked about how we are diminishing their power by treating them as such.

First, some fear or unsureness is normal, and their survival relies on it. However, we have seen dogs become increasingly fearful of household items and ordinary objects commonplace in the human world, which is very concerning. And not to mention very painful to see a dog so terrified of a vacuum, hairdryer, or someone wearing a hat. Oh, wait, other dogs? Or how about that scary balloon or, worse yet, nature's thunder? Sigh…

And worst of all, so many dogs have been doomed to fear things they don't need to, leaving humans to scramble to find answers from medication to thunder suits to trainers to trying to prevent what they fear from occurring. But we can't isolate them, which further creates fear in everything. Dogs are not meant to be isolated. They seek connection and purpose, just as we do.

I am not here to dispute that some legit trauma has occurred in many dogs' lives, leading them to be fearful and imbalanced. And for some, just plain ol' crappy breeding. And when you combine bad breeding (genetics) with a bad breeder (left isolated and unsure of the world) with more negative experiences throughout their life, rehabilitating these dogs can be incredibly difficult.

This book is not about those severe cases where so many things have been stacked against them. This book is about managing a younger dog's fear correctly, in the first place, so they do not have issues with unrealistic fears throughout their life.

An unrealistic fear is something your puppy does not need to fear. I promise the vacuum will not eat you. I promise the balloons are harmless. I promise you I will not allow anything to harm you. I promise you I would never ask you to do something you are not capable of.

Wait what? Can I empower my puppy to believe in me as their human leader? To trust me wholeheartedly? To know without a doubt that I will protect them, meet their needs, and provide a stable, loving home?

Yes. Yes, you can.

A critical difference in a breeder that has learned the Empowered Breeding program (and many have done so without my program) is that they raise their puppies to believe in their abilities and trust their first human hands and heart without question.

The Empowered Breeder program understands the sensitive developmental benchmarks of a puppy and how that needs to align with handling and exposure activities. We also understand our initial role is to gently assimilate ourselves into their life through the trust of their mama. It becomes a beautiful, unspoken relationship between us: human, mama, and *her* litter.

We don't assume we know best. We are there to support the first and most important relationship they have that will influence the rest of their life. And that is with their mama. So much like a human baby too.

Initial handling is gentle and brief. Puppies are only removed once briefly from their mama each day, and that is to weigh and perform a head-to-tail safety check. When we want to stroke or hold newborn puppies gently, it is done in the whelping box with their mama present. Puppies are born unable to see or hear and rely solely on their nose, so they can get very stressed if they can't smell her. We want content, well-fed, thriving puppies that have all their needs effortlessly met.

Around three weeks old, handling gets more structured (10-step handling exercises are performed) to introduce them to handling in a very respectful innate way. Eyes and ears are also open, so we begin gentle exposure to the world. Far too many breeders ruin their puppies at this age more than any other age. They push too fast. We must lay the foundation that everything we present to them is safe, fun, and that they are respected enough that they have the free will to engage or not while their nerve endings are still forming.

And what is also so important is that the exposure activity is done *in* the whelping box (novelty whelping box exposure activities). None of the activities are abrasive, unpredictable, or loud. Their nerve endings are far too sensitive, and the relationship between breeder and human is not firmly established enough for anything too unpredictable. We also employ the gift of the word "yes." If your puppy is not imprinted with this little gem, you can still teach them the power of yes!

As they explore, smell, and approach something new, we say "yes"! We are letting them know that this marker word means "yes", you can approach. "Yes", you are brave! "Yes", you can trust me. Then we give this gift to you to continue using, and boy, something so simple has massive positive effects.

When they are four weeks old (for medium and standard sized dogs – toys and minis are at least a week behind), we work them next to their whelping box building their resiliency, confidence, nerve strength, and trust. We still stay close to mama and the whelping box (all sounds and smells are the same), but we start to vary the items they are exposed to in a safe and empowering way. We cheerlead with "yes" and help guide emotional responses. If a puppy gets overwhelmed, we let them return to the safety of their whelping box and mama.

At five weeks and beyond, we work the puppies in different places. Puppies need to practice exploring new places. It dramatically affects their ability to be flexible and adaptable later in life. We vary the activities from unpredictable items, things with wheels, water, overhead exposures, textures, tactile footing, a neutral dog, problem solving practice, obstacle course challenges, new people, and brain games. Puppies are also exposed to many sounds ranging from different types of movies (a romance movie sounds very different from a war movie) to sounds of a vacuum to fireworks. It is important to note that puppies are highly situational when young. That means that the vacuum in my house is different from the vacuum in your house (not to mention different shapes, sizes, and sounds of vacuums), so some puppies will need to be reassured that it will, in fact, still not eat them.

Puppies are also specifically handled daily to create compliance with all sorts of touching. From ears to paws to their tail to their nails. They don't have to enjoy some of the "improper" handling, but they do have to learn to tolerate it. Having dogs that fear certain types of touching, clipping the nails, or being groomed is a huge disservice and unfair. So, teaching and practicing compliance is setting them up for a lifetime of less stress for the both of you.

Puppies not allowed to learn and grow in an empowering and safe environment can be disadvantaged. Everything we do is done with meaning and purpose.

Puppies learn that exploring the world is fun and they can believe in their abilities to encounter something new and maybe even a little scary at first. We are also there to practice startle recovery. It is ok if they startle at something. That is self-preservation, but it is vital that when we say "yes," they recover and investigate. Or at least shake it off and move on to something else. My goal is that they recover within three seconds of the initial startle. We do not rescue them. We do not swoop in and pick them up and coddle them. We do not enable them. We empower them. They have to go through the process to see that there is nothing to actually fear. If they don't, they have learned a valuable lesson: I should fear that. I am not capable. I cannot trust my humans to protect me from scary things.

And that is definitely not the lesson we want to tell our puppies. I know it is hard not to jump in and "save" them. But we must show them there is nothing to fear.

Now, I absolutely know there are things they should fear. Or at least have a healthy fear of it.
I am addressing unrealistic fears that then compile and lead to fearing more and more things like plastic bags, an umbrella, thunder, someone new coming in the house, the furniture moving, the dishwasher opening, their shadow, or even their reflection in the mirror (I can relate to this one, to be honest). Aging gracefully is a concept I am struggling with.
I have sent home nicely balanced puppies only to hear from their owner how they have grown increasingly fearful. This is sad for me to witness firsthand because I know that no matter how well-intentioned their humans are, fear was not handled properly as they grew. Their human truly felt they were doing the right thing by rushing in, removing the puppy from the situation, and consoling them. And then what comes next? We feel bad. And our puppy wonders why you are also feeling uncertain or struggling with guilt about that particular item or event, which negatively compounds the moment. It reinforces the feeling that they are not safe after all. You have confirmed to them that their fear was justified.

If you have done this, please don't beat yourself up. You are here.
Now.
Learning.

Wanting to do better.

And that is all that matters.

We can only do our best with the knowledge we have at the time.

So, what should you do when your puppy experiences an unrealistic fear?

• Stay neutral/keep a robust and safe composure.

• Use the "yes" empowerment word.

• Coax the puppy to investigate or at least move on to something else with ease (forward movement is powerful).

• Desensitize with the same object or noise over the next few days using treats/praise.

Let's go through some examples.

Since I already brought it up, let's talk about the dreaded vacuum.

Puppies display fear in two ways: fight or flight (sounds like another species I know) and they display their "fight" response by chasing, trying to bite, and barking.

Puppies with an exuberant amount of prey drive may actually be in play/prey drive, but either way, it needs to be addressed and stopped immediately. You let this slide, and then you could have a dog chasing bikes, kids, and other dogs (and not in a healthy way).

No thanks. No one wants that.

If you puppy chases the vacuum, do not allow that. If your puppy is fearful of the vacuum, it is time to handle that immediately. Start by desensitizing. Set the vacuum out in the front room and leave it there until the dog no longer cares about it. Move it to another spot. And another and make sure they no longer have any concern about it. Then turn it on randomly. Don't baby talk them or force them to investigate it (no pressure). Just turn on the vacuum and go about your business. They are watching you CLOSELY. And if you are not worried? Guess what? They won't be either. Once they don't care about the vacuum being on in random places, you can start pushing it around. You can toss treats there way or place fetch while pushing it around too. Distraction and forward movement are powerful. Just stay neutral and SHOW them there is nothing to fear, and you can do that essentially without saying a word.

If a puppy or grown dog has a negative experience, they must now experience 100 more positive experiences. Rather than trying to shield them from whatever scared them, they now need to have positive experiences over and over again. Our brain works the same way with fear.

For example, if another dog attacks your dog, you must get them back out safely as soon as possible (within days) to have positive encounters with dogs you know are balanced and friendly. Over and over again. Rewire that negative experience so it can no longer control their fear response. There are a few reasons I cringe at dog parks. One is ear mites, dog lice, giardia, roundworms, and mange (do I need to keep going)? It makes me feel like when I would cave in and let my kids play at the McDonald's ball pit. It was for selfish reasons too, I will admit. I could eat in PEACE, sit on my phone, or read a book, I didn't have to cook or clean, and the kids actually ate the food (even though it is crap, but tastes good). But let's be honest, those ball pits are gross…

Not only are there a lot of germs and the possibility of infections/lice, etc. I don't like dog parks because your dog runs in all happy to play, and all it takes is one jerk to ruin the mood. Your dog gets attacked, and you must run and break up a fight.

I always made sure I could climb my ass up into those McDonald's tunnels in case some kid was picking on my kid (or the other way around…I am a realist after all). All I have to say is that those tunnels are sticky… and small…and after having to do that once, I learned my lesson.

Dog parks can be fantastic if you know the dogs and the people... and if you can maintain your dog's safety. Enter at your own risk – a dog park and the McDonald's play center alike.

Chapter 10
Little Pals and Pups

I love watching children play with puppies! There's something so pure and innocent about their interactions. It's incredible to see the bond that forms between them and how much joy they bring to each other's lives.

Raising a child with a dog offers numerous benefits that contribute to their physical, social, and emotional development. One of the key advantages is the companionship and unconditional love dogs provide. Having a constant source of comfort, support, and emotional connection can be incredibly valuable for children as they navigate the ups and downs of life.

Caring for a dog also teaches children important life skills such as responsibility and empathy. From feeding and grooming to taking them for walks and playtime, children learn the importance of meeting a puppy's needs and understanding their emotions. This fosters a sense of empathy and compassion for others as they develop a deep connection with their puppy. They learn to understand and meet a dog's needs and recognize and respect their personal space. This valuable lesson in empathy extends beyond their interactions with dogs and can positively impact their relationships with other people.

Dogs naturally encourage physical activity and outdoor play. Whether going for walks, playing fetch, or engaging in other activities, the presence of a dog promotes exercise and contributes to a healthier lifestyle for both children and dogs. This physical engagement helps children develop stronger muscles, coordination, and overall fitness. This definitely helps in a world full of screens, video games and TV. Win for us!

Emotionally, dogs can have a significant impact on a child's well-being. Their presence has been shown to reduce stress, anxiety, and loneliness, offering a constant source of comfort and companionship. The bond between a child and their dog can provide a sense of security, helping them navigate challenging times with resilience and emotional support.

Interacting with dogs can also stimulate a child's cognitive development. From teaching them commands to problem-solving during playtime, dogs provide learning and cognitive engagement opportunities. Children develop memory, attention, and critical thinking skills, enhancing their overall cognitive abilities.

Whew, there are many compelling reasons why getting a dog for your children is beneficial but it's important to note that raising a child with a dog requires responsible pet ownership, proper supervision, and education on dog safety. Parents should create a safe and harmonious environment for the child and the dog, ensuring a mutually beneficial relationship.

Breeds with high energy levels, herding instincts, guarding instincts, higher prey drives and or a tendency to be more aggressive can be challenging for smaller children to handle. Parents must carefully research a breed's temperament before bringing a puppy into a household with young children. When you bring home a puppy, kids must also be trained. It can be one of the most challenging aspects of raising a puppy and children together, but the reward of watching them grow and bond is undoubtedly worth it.

The way small children move, and sound is *just* like a littermate, and let's be perfectly clear…the way they treat one another is not how you want one to treat your child. They chase, bite and pounce on one another. They are practicing their hunting skills!

Puppies love a game of chase and squeal. It will ignite their prey and play drive and GAME ON. They will pounce, mouth (bite), and "attack"! Just as their instincts tell them to. It is absolutely one of the most fun things a puppy can do.

The more they "attack," the more kids scream, which tells the puppy that this is precisely what they should be doing! Parents get frustrated, puppies get deemed "bad," and kids are full of scratches, teeth marks, and countless clothes left with holes.

How is the puppy managed now? Left outside more? Put in a kennel more than they should? This only makes the game MORE fun since they have pent-up energy and frustration since their needs are not being met. You can see how this is truly a problem. And at fault? You, the adult.

I am here to help! Here are three crucial rules when adding a puppy to a family with children.

The first is, ***"Don't make a peep, let the puppy sleep!"***

It's important to remember that puppies need lots of sleep. Ensure your child understands that the puppy needs quiet time and should not be disturbed while sleeping. No laying on them, poking at them, pulling at them, or trying to wake them up. Puppies that do not get enough sleep do get crabby and throw tantrums. We need puppies to get enough rest, so we prevent them from becoming overstimulated and potentially misbehave. Overtired puppies become restless and are more likely to act out. Providing them with a comfortable place to sleep and allowing them to rest when they need to, is crucial for their overall health and behavior. And your sanity as well!

The second rule we call is, *"Freeze like a tree?"*

Your more assertive drivey puppies will challenge "the tree" more, so if you took home a puppy with that aptitude, it is up to you to step it up a notch. Some breeds are more challenging with smaller children, as are some puppies with certain traits. Regardless, when a puppy is jumping or biting or tying to chase your child, teach them to freeze like a tree and ignore the puppy! Have them place their hands under their armpits and turn their backside to the puppy. If the puppy jumps, barks, or keeps running around to their front side, stay firm and turn slowly, facing away from the puppy. It won't take long, and the puppy will know your child no longer wants to engage. This is especially useful when the puppy is playing inappropriately.

Also, please watch how your child plays with the puppy. Are they "teasing" the puppy with the toy or their hand? This behavior trains the puppy to jump higher and bite harder to get the toy/hand that keeps getting dangled in front of their face and pulled away. This type of play with a puppy will actually make puppies fairly assertive in grabbing something from your child's hand. And then they wonder why they were scolded for such behavior when they were trained to do that exact thing.

Our third rule is *"Sit Like a Statue!"*

Children can also overhandle puppies, leaving some to feel like they must fend for themselves. Low growls when they get picked up can be one sign of this. Another is that the puppy tries to avoid the child, but their attempts to get some free space and time is ignored, so teach your child to sit like a "statue" in the middle of the floor with some puppy toys. They can't move. The puppy gets to decide when they approach, where they move, which toys to play with, and how to play (fetch, tug, etc.). The puppy also decides if they want to lay in their lap. If the puppy is jumping at their face or biting your child, instruct your child to stand up and "freeze like a tree." Once the behavior stops, your child can sit back down. I would not play this game if your puppy were having the zoomies or is over-excited. We want calm and appropriate play between both. We want to give our puppies free play too, so they don't feel like they have lost all their free will. It is important that they have some say on how to play and what to play with. Equally important is when they say they want to play alone, that is respected. This can be especially important if they were given a bone or other high value treat item to gnaw away at.

One great way to have a "safe" kid-free place to sleep or chew is to kennel train your puppy. Make the kennel a hands-off area for kids. It is an important boundary to make and will help teach your kids about respecting the puppy's personal space and time too. If you have several children, please monitor to ensure there is not constant handling. Our dear puppies will try to keep up with a busy family, but they do so at the cost of their well-being. And what a great lesson to teach our children: dogs need to be able to trust us. They need their innate needs met. We need to lead with consideration, kindness, and respect. Future partners of your child will thank you too.

Chapter 11
Whatcha Saying?

I have a secret.

There are many ways to train, communicate with, and correct a dog.

Shocking, I know. But I feel a massive weight off my shoulders for being able to divulge this necessary information. So, if just a part of this works for you and your dog, I have done my job.

Ok wait. I have one more secret before I can move on. Calling it a secret makes it sound forbidden or wrong. So, let's say a disclosure of sorts.

Deep breath, Jeanette. You have come this far. What is one more thing to permanently put on paper? In a book?

I am speaking from my truth.
My experience.
My gift of being able to communicate with dogs.
And dogs need *consequences* for inappropriate behavior.

There I said it.

I have observed dogs and puppies since my childhood. I have trained facility dogs, therapy dogs, and service dogs. I have rehabbed rescue dogs. And most importantly, I have raised hundreds of puppies (please don't automatically cringe at that thought). The beauty in this is that I have experience. I have failed. Learned. Succeeded. And failed more. But I also have knowledge and lots of experience. As you could so eloquently say, I have been around the block a few times.

For naysayers and those with different opinions and experiences (positive only training), I do not discount your journey. I do not spend my life energy attacking others. I choose to continue to say what I have to say.

What I believe in. What I have witnessed and learned. What I am still learning and what I know to be my truth when I sit in the same space with a dog.

Completely and with clarity.

Without force.

Without dictatorship.

But instead, with love, respect, and fairness.

Complete peace.

It is when I truly feel whole.

Understood.

First, I must stress that dogs are not all the same. Whether the breed or the specific puppy. They are not robots created by a model and then mass-produced. They are living and thinking beings. They have been or will be shaped by their life experiences and inevitably become a product of that. And guess what? The same applies to us!

Standing up for yourself, being consistent, being fair, and genuinely committing to raising a puppy is essential in making this successful.

But this is also what makes this topic complicated.

For real.

Many variables can come into play. And for this book. This chapter. I am solely focusing on "normal" puppy behaviors that need to be guided/corrected/reprimanded. See how even the word I use; you instantly feel one is far more comfortable for you? You will find that correcting a puppy will also have variables that feel more comfortable to you. I will address this as we move through this chapter, considering every puppy is different. Every human is different. Every human-puppy bond is different.

Whew, this was an undertaking.

Stay with me here!

Choosing a puppy or older dog that aligns with your personality and considering your strengths and weaknesses is vital to a happy and healthy relationship with your dog. But also important is being able to communicate effectively with your puppy. My focus on this topic is about bringing home a new puppy, which could also apply to bringing home an older puppy/dog. I am not addressing dogs that need *severe behavior* modification.

I will talk about guiding, shaping, and molding your puppy into a compliant (most of the time), respectful (most of the time) puppy where you can lay down some necessary rules and expectations for the betterment of your puppy. A puppy that grows into a dog that becomes a productive member of society. A dog that has a healthy understanding of who the boss is and that if they do something that is not accepted in your house, there will be consequences.

The funny thing about consequences for a dog (and people, quite honestly) is that if they are not uncomfortable enough, then there is no reason not to keep doing the unwanted behavior to begin with. Secondly, if we are not correctly communicating the expectations to our puppy, we cannot hand out consequences nor expect them to understand what the heck we are asking of them in the first place.

As a responsible dog owner, it is crucial to distinguish between normal and unacceptable behavior in your puppy. Common behaviors that require guidance, correction, or reprimand include inappropriate chewing / biting (people), jumping on people, resource guarding, counter surfing, and excessive barking. Consequences for unacceptable actions must be uncomfortable enough for the puppy to learn from the experience without inducing fear or anxiety. Firmly saying "no" and using your body to show them "no" by standing tall and still (have the presence that you mean business) is highly successful as long as your timing and presence is on point. It is not what you say but how you "say" it.

Case and point. And this is a fun one. Let's say you don't want your dog on the couch. Right? They jump up on the couch; you say no. You grab their collar and pull them down.

They jump back up again. You repeat until you give in, confident your dog is untrainable. Too stubborn. Maybe even a little bit dumb.

From your puppy's point of view: This is an annoying interaction you have with them.

"Oh, here we go again…up. Down. Up. Down. Up…and…wait for it. Nothing?
Yes! I can finally curl up and sleep."

One of three things is happening:
1. You don't know how to communicate with your dog.
2. Inconsistency. Sometimes you're firm enough that they respond and listen to you; other times, you are not.
3. One person in the house allows the dog on the couch, and the other person does not (this is not fair).

How about barking at people walking by? You have this beautiful large front room window that initially attracted you to the house, to begin with. The beautiful morning sunlight fills the room with warmth and happiness each day.

Until you got a dog.

Now you hate that dang window and wish people would just walk a different route. Is there any reason they need to walk by *your* window everyday anyway? There are plenty of other routes available. Take another one, for crying out loud.
Pretty Please?

So, your dog barks. You yell, "Quiet." Your dog does not listen to you. The barking continues.

And some of you have been given this special gift of tuning it out. You carry on like the dog is not even barking! How is this even possible? I still am amazed, quite frankly.
And then there are others (admittedly like me) that do not like barking. The sudden startle. The LOUD production. The nonsense that ensues.
And most importantly, is the dog's state of mind when in these barking frenzies is just not healthy.

I value and appreciate my dog's bark if someone tries to enter my home. Or property. But I need them to understand I can take it from there when I say 'quiet.' I've got it. They do *not* need to worry, protect and worse, enter a frenzied state of mind by someone entering my house or, even better, simply walking by my window.

But we give in. Give up. And even just accept it.

From your puppy's point of view, they bark. You bark (by yelling quiet).

Great.

We all bark.

That is not the message you were trying to convey. But you are.

OK, one more for fun!

Your dog chases the cat. And for that matter, it could be a bike or kids. But we will talk about our feline friends for the sake of simplicity.

If you are lucky, your cat won't take that crap from a puppy and stand their ground. It may look like flipping their tail around. Growling. Swatting at the puppy with their paws (maybe even claws out). And they for sure as heck don't run. Why? A puppy, without a doubt, will chase. Period. End of story. Best game ever. They repeat as much as necessary to establish the puppy FULLY understands what will and what will not be allowed. And, just like that, beautiful boundaries are laid. Over time, cats and dogs often become friends and live happily ever after. It is fascinating to witness a cat communicating correctly with a puppy.

If your cat does not stand their ground, what options do you have? Because we know that the cat will outrun the dog, and inevitably, this game will become less and less fun because they never catch the cat (the reward). And let's be clear. We are talking about a normal puppy PLAY drive. If you see signs or are concerned that their play seems far more intense and you are worried about your cat's safety, seek professional help immediately. I have rarely seen (and not at all in my breeding program) an 8-week-old puppy have intentions other than play. It is also important to note that you should proceed with absolute CAUTION if you bring in an older dog.

Back to a typical mischievous puppy whose FAVORITE game is…. chase. You got it.

Cat runs. Game on. If they collide, the puppy tackles the cat like a littermate. But believe me, and you understand this if you have a cat too, that a cat rarely likes that type of play. Some do. They are rare, and for most, it takes time for the cat to teach the puppy how they are willing to play.

It is hard to watch a new puppy chase your cat constantly. You feel bad because your once social cat is now in hiding, like in a top-level witness protection type of hiding. So, when the puppy chases the cat, you join in running after the puppy while saying, "Stop chasing the cat"!

From the puppy's point of view? They turn around and see that you have joined the fun game of chasing the cat and couldn't be more delighted.

Sure, being the coolest owner feels good, but not quite the message you were going for.

Oh, the woe of inappropriately communicating with your puppy. See how much we misinterpret and misunderstand each other? This is a disaster setting you up for failure.

So, how do you communicate your expectations clearly so you can have a home with healthy boundaries, rules, and limitations? We know it is necessary and that their innate needs must be met to have a balanced and fulfilled dog.

Let's break this down as simple as possible, keeping in mind that every puppy is different, as are children, and so many variables could play out. What is important is that you understand you may need to practice if this is your first puppy or if you have a more challenging puppy. Don't give up if the puppy does not respond to your correction. Keep trying. Improving. Tweaking. Revising.

In almost every case I have seen where the puppy was not listening despite these steps being followed, it was because the human didn't ***mean*** it. They didn't have the right "authority" vibe. And a puppy is more than happy to call your bluff. As are our kids. Same same.

First, you cannot expect a puppy to "just do something" when you have not trained, reinforced, practiced, praised, or set them up for success. When we bring home a puppy, it is our oath and duty to ensure we have the time, energy, and patience to teach this puppy the necessary *life skills* to be empowered.

The first essential part of communicating with a puppy is interrupting the THOUGHT before they move into action. You are too late if the puppy is already doing the behavior/action. If you continue to be "too late" and miss the THOUGHT before they spring into action, you need to get a handle on this. Prevention and redirection are key. This alone will reduce so much frustration in your relationship. If your puppy is jumping up on the couch, and you cannot interrupt the thought before any paws leave the ground, it is only fair to prevent access to the couch until you can commit to the actual training. We often assume a dog knows how to walk on a leash, not jump on people, or to not get on a couch.

Teach and guide them through respect; you must catch them thinking about it. So as the puppy goes over to the couch and right before paws leave the ground (like it is evident they are going to jump on the couch or at least attempt a go at it), you interrupt the thought of that behavior by a quick clap and sharp "No"! Rules, boundaries, and limitations are an innate need for a puppy/dog to thrive, so please do not feel bad. They will feel safer and more secure by understanding the rules, having structure, and being guided through fairness. The second part of the "correction" is to stand, freeze, and or body block (stand between the couch and the puppy). If they try to move toward the couch still (and the longer they have been allowed to jump on the couch, the longer this process will take) you must stand your ground and block them with your body. Limit your words and use your body as nonverbal communication. Once the puppy relents, you walk away. Message received. Be ready though, they may try again immediately or in a few minutes. And of course, again tomorrow.

The critical thing to remember is that just like kids (and some adults, for that matter), they will test boundaries. They will make sure you mean it. So, make sure you are consistent! Very very consistent. It is a lot of work in the first year. But the goal is that you have laid the foundation and built a relationship based on respect so that anytime in the future, a simple "no" will mean stop. Stop whatever they are going to do, no matter where they are and what they are thinking about doing.

Stop that thought about chasing the cat. Stop that thought about taking the food off the counter. Stop that thought before barking. Stop that thought about leaping out of the car until permission is granted (teaching the wait command can come in nicely here).

As a reminder, effectively communicating with a puppy interrupts the thought of doing something before they do it. And then you need to follow through (stand your ground literally) to guarantee the puppy understands you mean business. Period.

Regardless of your house rules, every dog must be assimilated into our society. They adjust. They learn. They grow. They thrive. But if left to do whatever they want whenever they want, we get dogs left without a compass. A life vest. A safety net and Lord knows we all want to feel SAFE in our relationships.

When puppy raising, most interactions should be managed through prevention and redirection, and very little correcting should even be done. "No" should not become their name. For every correction, there should be 100 praises of affirmation. So often, we find ourselves entangled in a relationship where we say "no," take things from their mouth 100 times a day, chase them around, save our kids from shark teeth, and clean up pee for the third time. All before lunchtime.

Puppy raising is not easy work, especially if you put in the necessary work to have a balanced dog that is a productive member of society.
One that lives harmoniously with their human counterparts.
One that is empowered and feels safe.

Having a respectful relationship with your dog takes work. It is earned through dedication, consistency, fairness, and love. It should not and cannot be an "equal" relationship. Having presence and leadership is needed for a dog to thrive. A dog that can do as it pleases when they want, disregarding manners and engaging in appropriate behavior, is unfair. It is a recipe for disaster and before you know it, you start making excuses for your dog's ill behavior.

An empowered puppy is a happy puppy. They feel understood and safe. Rules are fair and leadership is consistent and kind. What a great way to be raised. Not only for our puppies but for our children too.

"I receive lots of praise. My innate needs are met in order. I don't have many chances to fail. I am set up to succeed and be guided safely through expectations. I am taught the rules in my home and know the consequences. There is no ambivalence about my health and safety. I am given every opportunity for play, curiosity, problem-solving, and learning. I am praised when I do things well and feel pride in myself.
I am understood.
Honored.
Respected.
Valued.

And I am reassured when I waiver.

I am loved unconditionally".

Every puppy in the world is saying, "YES! Please sign me up! Could you give me that human? The one that understands?"

Don't worry, little peanut. I am working on it. For all of you.

Chapter 12
The Power 3

There are three things every puppy should experience during puppy raising and beyond, and I call them the Power 3. They can transform your relationship with your puppy, catapulting you into the next level of your relationship far faster. They can teach focus and self-control, two things some never learn. And what a shame that is. Why are we not helping our dogs practice and master both? Self-control and focus are necessary lifelong skills. Dogs don't deserve to be agitated, anxious, or fearful.

Some working dogs need to be in a different state of mind. I am not referring to those exceptions; however, all working dogs still must display excellent focus and self-control even if in an excited state of mind to work. I am referencing reliable family companions. And for the first time, creating a unity, a connection, a program where breeders, dogs, and owners are all on the same page for the same mission - to have healthier, happy dogs. And that is all there is to it.

1. Sit on the Dog

The first in the Power 3 series is "The Sit on the Dog" activity. I cannot take credit for who started this training exercise, but it is brilliant, and you will reap HUGE rewards with minimal effort. That is a win-win in my book, and while we are talking about books, just because it is now in print, in the hands of every dog owner (one can hope, right?), I can no longer keep this exercise a secret between you and me. After all, you will have the best-behaved dog you can take anywhere and have EVERYONE commenting on how well-behaved your dog is. And that feels GOOD, but a small smile creeps across your face as you have used this easy method to get there! This tip. This gift. And, boy, did it pay off, and they had *no idea* how easy this was.

All you have to do is sit and ignore your puppy. That is it. I promise. I will even pinky promise. But you do need to follow these fundamental rules to make certain its ultimate success.

You must ignore your puppy. I know. I know. But I believe in you; your dog needs you to do this for them. You are not actually sitting on your dog. I should have led with that before I asked you to pinky promise. You are sitting on their leash. Or have the leash clipped to your belt loop ("coupler" leash or add a carabiner on one end). Or even a hands-free leash that goes around your waist.

Make sure there is nothing your puppy can get into. Sit in a safe place and have something to do. Watch TV. Sit at your computer. Sit and read a book. Sit and eat dinner (if it will be acceptable for you to have the dog in the kitchen by the table).

Side note, while we are talking about the dinner table. Take it or leave it but look at it from the dog's point of view and not the way it makes you feel good to "spoil" them. Do not feed your dog from the table. Ever. Otherwise, you get a dog begging for food, which is just not good manners. If you want to give them a special treat from your plate, wait to finish dinner and give it to them in another area. It is unfair to "train" a dog to constantly beg for the next scrumptious bite. Now? Now? You? How about you? Now? Now? Please. Whine. Pace. Around and around, they go.

Back to the sit on the dog exercise. The first time you do this with your puppy they will very likely resist confinement. They have not successfully practiced this skill. And if they are older and have never had the opportunity or human that believed in them enough to teach them how to self-soothe, settle and be 'OK' in the space with you, be ready. I can relate to this on many levels. I have a hard time being still and letting my brain settle. Meditation is torture for me. Why the heck do I want to be alone with my thoughts? But I am also working on this for personal growth. For a happier state of mind. For my health. And our dogs deserve to be afforded the same opportunity.

Do **not** stop the exercise if your pup throws a fit. If you do, you have just taught them that they have a say and don't have to do what you want. Uh…not the lesson we are going for here. Think about things in your life that are good for you, and you resisted at first, and now you are thankful that someone else made you do it and or you stuck with it. Your dog will thank you. Unequivocally.

Let them alligator roll. Scream. Sit at the very end of the leash with tension. Let them pout. Let them simmer. Let them keep the pressure on the leash for as long as they need. This is an important process for them, and I have had puppies give in just barely, at the end of the leash, with slight tension on it. I just have to smile at the strong-headedness I am in for and remind myself that I am in fact more determined. I won't let them fail. I will show them, I can lead, and they can trust me. Then I take a deep breath and steel myself for what will come.

I can't help but be reminded of raising my son. He is 17 now and was the most strong-willed, stubborn child. Off the charts. I thought he would break me. He is still both of those things, but now having a son on the brink of adulthood is very different from having a toddler. Or a kindergartner when I am was trying to get him to do his homework. Never would I think sitting down with my blue-eyed, blonde, curly hair son to help him with his ABCs would be pure hell. No mom is prepared for that. But boy or boy. Every school night became a war zone. He had resisted boundaries, rules, chores, and, quite frankly, anything he hasn't wanted to do. I often wondered; how has this child could come from me? I am a natural rule follower. I don't like constant confrontation. I will do what is asked of me and without trouble (usually). I spent many nights crying and wondering how I had failed him so badly. What was I doing wrong? I read every parenting book I could get my hands on and tried every new approach I would read about. Uh… not sure whom they were writing about, but that didn't work. Put him on timeout until he was willing to do his homework. He would sleep. Make a positive chart so he can earn rewards. He would quickly decide he didn't like Chuck E Cheese, ice cream, Pokémon cards or anything else on that chart for that matter.

Great.

I spent a great deal of time wondering if I was capable of raising him. But I learned that I was never going to change him, and I also began to value and admire his strong will (in most situations) because I saw strength. I saw someone willing to stand up for himself. Someone with deep beliefs about things and who was unwilling to change his mind every 30 seconds because someone else says or does something different. I have done my best to adjust my parenting to meet his needs while also trying to instill an understanding of the greater good.

Respect. Kindness. Love.

And there will always be things we do not want to do in life, but we have to anyway.

There have been compromises. Arguments. Hurtful things have been said. There have been times I have felt like a complete failure to him and myself. But I haven't given up, and while no relationship is perfect and no person is perfect, we have blossomed as mother and son, and despite our differences, we have a lot in common too.

So, when I deal with those puppies who always want to have the last word and do things their own way, I remind myself that they've got their own personality too. And while I may get some things wrong, I will continue to work to find training methods that work. I will continue to seek correction levels and communication that make sense to that puppy. And I will continue to honor them for who they are and not try to make them something they are not. I will also remember that this puppy, like EVERY puppy, needs rules, boundaries, and limitations. I remind myself that I have already been trained, primed, and ready for this battle (thank you son). So, bring it on.

If you want to sleep at the very end of the leash. Go ahead, Peanut. Knock yourself out. I see you. But I also love you enough and care about your mental health for the rest of your life, so before you know it, you will be curled up at my feet sleeping. Content. Feeling safe. And understanding, this girl doesn't mess around. And when these little milestones happen, a shift in our relationship occurs. Respect is being built. It is my duty. My oath. My commitment as a dog owner to you is that you understand who is in charge and what is expected of you. And by doing that, I take a lot of weight off your shoulders. No need to worry. I've got you.

Let them figure out that the pressure of the leash releases when they come close to you. This is so important. They learn that the release of pressure is when they are next to you. How powerful is that? So, hang in there. Each lesson will get easier and easier. Once they settle down, start a timer. Thirty minutes of calm behavior, whether sleeping or quietly chewing on a bone, is needed before you can end the session.

They may bite at the leash. A quick snap of the leash and "no" and ignore. Repeat, if necessary, but if you find that is all you are doing, you will create a puppy that thinks their name is "No" and, even worse, a puppy that ignores minor corrections. After all, your corrections were not unpleasant enough to stop doing it. If you find yourself in this position, get a high-value bone (raw - not cooked, plastic, natural, kong, etc.). With anything you give your dog, please research, and monitor carefully to avoid choking and or diarrhea. I look for something that they cannot ingest easily, if at all. And, of course, keeping in mind items that could crack their teeth. Anything thin and dense enough to fit behind their molars can crack a tooth. If I get antlers, I get thicker ones. I like larger bully sticks. I place it in a Ziploc in between exercises. I cannot recommend rawhide due to the higher chance of choking. Regardless of what you use, there is always a risk: choking, diarrhea, blockage, and cracked teeth. Use at your own discretion. As they age, the need for something to chew on during this exercise will wane.

If you can get your puppy to settle without a distraction, that is ideal. But some puppies are very mouthy; however, if I find a puppy that can't keep his mouth off me, the leash, or the leg of the chair, I will mitigate by upping the exercise and mental stimulation combined with more chewing on appropriate things before even starting this exercise! Meeting their needs is respectful and responsible.

Do not set young puppies up to fail by doing this exercise at the height of their energy. Not cool at all. Meet their needs in order and when it is nap time, take advantage of a quiet moment for both of you and grab the leash.

Once your puppy displays mastery by quickly going into their long down stay, settling in nicely, displaying self-control, and the ability to be content, it is time to start varying the places you sit.
Start with everywhere possible in your house and the backyard/patio area. Then the front yard. At first, with little distraction. Depending on where you live, these times could vary.

Ok, time to ramp up the distraction slowly and respectfully. You cannot expect a puppy to go from your house to outside Wal-Mart. Or a bench outside a busy playground. Or an outdoor cafe.

You get the idea.

Build distraction and duration in this exercise. The duration begins with an 8-week-old puppy for 30 minutes after they settle. If you add distraction, wait to add duration. Remember, we are setting our puppies up for success, not to fail.

Once you build a solid foundation in newer places, you can slowly start trying more unpredictable places. When other people are in the equation, you must not let them pet your dog. Remember the ignore rule? It applies to strangers, family, and friends. Why the heck am I so rude and mean? Let me tell you. For my dog. And for the hard work, we have already put in.

Do you want strangers to come up and pet you?
Maybe you are happy about this idea. And maybe not.
Just like our dogs.

Look at the mindset shift that could happen if you *do not* want the unwarranted petting. We went from calm and safe to feeling anxious and unsettled. Or if they LOVE meeting new people, it creates excitement and then that excitement is rewarded by the stranger petting them. Oh boy, this isn't good either.

Everything we have worked so hard for is gone. We have retrained our dog to be anxious or excited, and not content and calm. This is one of the exact reasons you should never talk to, pet, or give a service dog attention. You are untraining their dog. And now, instead of focusing on their handler, they are looking to everyone else for attention.

2. Hand feeding

Feeding a dog is an event that we overlook the power of too often. In our society, everything revolves around food, sometimes even our emotions.

When someone dies, food is served.

When someone celebrates a Birthday, food is served.

When someone finds out they are pregnant, food is served.

When someone reveals the gender of their baby, food is served.

When someone gets married, food is served.

Holidays? Food is served.

And guess what? There are now divorce parties, and food is served.

People gather in good times and bad—a chance to share life and connection over food. We have a highly complex system. Food is a means of identifying and retaining our cultural identity. It is a powerful way to connect with like-minded people who have shared similar life experiences. A means to bring a feeling of something like being "homesick" seeping right out of our hearts with the whiff of one dish. Memories flood back. Feelings are overwhelming. We are forced voluntarily or involuntarily to deal with that emotional flood right then and there.

Food has become love, a way to connect, a way to hide, a chance to create, and an opportunity to find joy. Food allows us to seek a universal understanding.

Food is powerful in our human culture. It is one thing that unites us despite ALL our millions of differences.

Feeding your dog entails opening a bag of kibble, scooping out a premeasured amount, and placing it on the floor.

Chore done. Check.

Wait a minute. Not so fast. I know we have 100 things or more to do in a day, but when raising a new puppy, one way to connect with them on a deeper level is? You guessed it, food.

Hand Feeding your puppy will have a long-lasting, powerful effect on your relationship. Those that provide food to a dog are held to a higher standard. I mean, I feel the same way. If someone shopped, made, and prepared my food for me, I would freaking hold them in HIGH regard.

So, let's agree to take advantage of this opportunity.

Food plays a crucial role in the canine world, serving as a source of sustenance and a means of nourishment, health, and connection. Beyond nutrition, food holds significant social and emotional value for dogs. Mealtime becomes a moment of anticipation and enjoyment, fostering a sense of routine, comfort, and security. Sharing meals with their human companions strengthens the bond between them, as dogs instinctively associate food-related interactions with love, care, and affection. Furthermore, using food as a training tool promotes positive reinforcement, enhancing learning and strengthening communication between dogs and their owners.

This type of information is valuable in further understanding and monopolizing how I manage feeding time with my dogs, ensuring it is done with meaning and purpose.

One way to lay the foundation of the concept of food comes from me as the leader, your protector, and your parent (so to speak) is to hand feed or have their attention when food is given. Hand feeding is largely beneficial. You also guarantee the focus is on you and not just the food. And one of the other significant benefits is the opportunity to work with your dog while handing out the reward of food. Nothing in life is for free, and that philosophy should be carried on to how you treat your dog. When they earn things, they feel more fulfilled and balanced. This concept reminds me of when I was in college. It was common to see those students who had their parents paying for everything not take college as seriously. They had no skin in the game, and many kids, don't appreciate or value anything when things are handed to them.

Instead, I would instill a positive working relationship with my dogs and give them many opportunities to "work" for things they need or want.

Balance.

Stability.

A sense of accomplishment.

Empowerment.

Belief in their own abilities.

Hand feeding can be used in various ways, so let's explore that now!

First, it sounds just like it is. You hand-feed your puppy. But to maintain its purpose, there are a few things to know.

1. Please only feed them if you ask for something in return. It could be as simple as eye contact, sitting or following you. Remember to ensure you are not rewarding excitement or inappropriate behaviors.

2. You can feed a handful at a time or just a few pieces of kibble. Or even set the whole bowl down if you are in a rush. But make sure you asked something of them. You connected.

3. To continue to have an adaptable dog, mix it up! Where and how you feed should be changed up! Otherwise, you could get a puppy that will only eat out of your hand or one that will only eat out of a particular bowl.

4. To advance their self-control and focus, you can ask your puppy to "wait" before approaching any food. And then give them permission to eat.

5. If your puppy eats roughly from your hand, teach them to "be nice." I close my hand around the food if their teeth touch my skin. They can lick and smell, and as soon as they stop using their teeth, I open back up my hand, letting them hand feed. I say, "Be nice," as they eat nicely from my hand. Repeat as many times as needed in one sitting or for each meal. Be consistent, and in no time, you will have a dog that you never have to worry about being rough when taking food from a hand. The "be nice" command is handy if a small

child gives your dog a treat in the future too. It reminds them to be soft-mouthed and gentle when taking something from a human's hand.

6. Perform some variation of hand feeling for at least four weeks. When your puppy hits sexual maturity and starts rechallenging you (not all do), implement again to reestablish and remind your adolescent dog how things will be done in your home.

7. Use hand feeding with tether training when feeling super ambitious and have the time. Younger puppies will only be able to give you this amount of focus for a shorter period, so as soon as you see they are struggling with focus, end on a positive note and then feed them the rest of their food in a bowl. A fanny pack or training pouch on your right hip and leash on the left. Randomly, name and reward (with their food) a behavior. An example of this is if they sit. As soon as they do, say "sit" and give them a piece of kibble (or training treat for an older pup). I love catching and praising/rewarding when they do something great! They also feel so good about themselves. This gives you such a positive environment of training and communication that is essential to the health of your relationship.

If you choose to feed raw, you can use smaller amounts of food in a bowl for training /focus sessions.

The ultimate goal is for your puppy to think you hung the moon and stars. You are their personal cheerleader, paparazzi, and Pez dispenser. But only if they earned it by being brave, working hard and exhibited self-control and focus!

3. Tether Training

The third practice in the Power 3 is tether training. This is a highly beneficial way to bond and foster trust between you and your dog. You see, like in any relationship, trust is the anchor. When you cannot trust someone, other behaviors are exhibited. In dogs, that is anxiousness and or aggression. Imagine if you literally had a lifeline handed to you, and it was a physical and metaphorical "cord" that meant safety, security, and trust. An anchor. Something that genuinely represents the ideology that I can be brave. I don't have to worry about anything, and I can honestly believe in myself because I cannot fail.

That is what a leash can mean.

That a what a leash *should* mean.

It shouldn't ultimately mean containment or control. But instead, their lifeline. The reminder that you will provide, protect, and honor them above all else.

That level of connection does come with rules and boundaries. And one of those is that a leash must be a positive "connection" and not something that brings frustration and resistance (pulling).

Tether training is the holy grail to lay this foundation. It will take some time and practice but will have life-changing effects with consistency and patience.

The rules are pretty simple (thank goodness). You will be "tethering" the dog to you via its leash. There are a few ways to do this. You can buy a "hands-free" leash many use for jogging or service dog work. You can buy a "coupler" with clips on both sides (one for the dog collar and one for your belt loop) or put a carabiner on the leash and connect it to you. How you make the tethering happen is less important than what you do when the dog is tethered to you.

Here are a few guidelines:

Gradually increase the time the dog is tethered to you, and use positive reinforcement techniques, such as treats and praise, to encourage good behavior. It's important never to leave the dog tethered to you for extended periods of time, especially when they are younger.

1. Tether training a dog involves using a 4-6 foot leash to keep the dog close to you while allowing them some freedom to move around. The tether should be long enough to allow the dog to lie down and move around comfortably but not so long that they can move too far away from you.
2. Young puppies cannot be tethered to you. Depending on the breed and size of the puppy, you may need to wait to implement tether training. They must be bigger and more coordinated to keep up with you.
3. The goal is not to tug and pull at the puppy but to have the puppy naturally want to follow you. Praise and reward for them staying close to you. When they pull, simply stop, and wait for them to come back and investigate you. Then reward like crazy! But start with short (just a few minutes a day) lessons and build as they can be tethered for extended periods.
4. When you begin tether training, please don't have things you must do around the house. It takes time for the puppy or dog to understand what you want and need from them. And this will lead to frustration as you

trip around the puppy and the leash as you figure out what the heck is going on. You want to reinforce and teach the puppy to stay next to you and move with you seamlessly. After time and practice, it becomes a beautiful unspoken dance between human and dog.

5. Name and reward when they do things you want. If they look at you? Say, "Watch Me," and reward. If they sit, say, "Sit," and reward them immediately. When you begin tether training, you can't be distracted by other things. Let this be a time for training and building a relationship. One with mutual respect. Dogs do not just naturally know what you want. We can't punish or expect something we have not taught/expressed or rewarded.

Chapter 13
All Eyes on Me

Something so simple but profound is that your dog can only focus on *ONE* thing at a time. Ok, I hear you thinking, "How in the heck is that so profound, Jeanette?"

Because.

Amazing things happen if we change our mindset from fighting to keep their attention to laying the foundation from the beginning. By implementing everything I have talked about the Power 3, handling fear correctly, socializing with respect and kindness, meeting their needs in order, consistency, fairness, and setting them up for success, we are making ourselves very valuable.

You are given a gift when a dog feels safe with you and truly trusts you implicitly. They give themselves to you completely. This is the same in a human-to-human relationship. When actions match words, and we know exactly where we stand and have nothing, but a relationship built on respect, we are well on our way to being their main focus (despite what is happening in the environment). Now, don't think there is not still more work to do. We have to practice and "proof" their self-control and focus. We must continue managing emotional responses in and out of the house.

For example, I will work a young puppy out in front of my house (vaccines taken into consideration). There can be so many distractions. Cars are driving by, the neighbor is walking their dog, or a kid is riding their bike. Yes! So many opportunities to reinforce a few important things.

1. Nothing bad will happen to you. I am here.
2. Look at me; I will reassure and praise/treat you if needed.
3. There is no response needed other than a neutral demeanor. Nothing to be excited about. Nothing to fear. Nothing to react to.

You have already been empowered with the command "yes" and have been teaching and guiding leash work, emphasizing not pulling and staying close to you. This behavior is reinforced by rewarding them with treats and using the command "heel" when their head or nose is positioned right at your left leg.

Remember, they can only focus on one thing at a time, and what I want my dog to know without a doubt is that no matter what is happening around us, if they stay focused on me, good things happen. I am a Pez dispenser, after all. The giver and not the taker. We are too quick to always take things away and by doing that we add value to those items. I want the value to be on me.

A car drives by? If needed, I say "Yes" and their name, and then instantly give them a treat. I am conditioning them that there is NO concern with cars. And by giving *me* their focus, they are rewarded.

When I notice the neighbor approaching with their dog during a walk, as soon as I see that my dog has spotted them, I say, "Yes," to grab their attention and offer them a treat. This action reinforces the idea that we should not respond or react to other people or dogs. My goal is to establish a sense of neutrality, where my dog remains unconcerned about external distractions and focuses on me during our walk without getting bothered by unnecessary distractions.

When a child rides by on their bike and my dog becomes alert, with ears perked and focused on them, I intervene *before* my dog reacts. Timing is crucial in this situation. I promptly request my dog's attention and reward it immediately before they have a chance to respond to the bike. I ask for their focus and then provide a reward. However, if I am too late and my dog has already shifted from noticing and processing to reacting or moving, I recognize that I missed the opportunity. In such cases, I can pivot and move away from the child on the bike. I may place a high value treat in front of my dog's nose. I can stand still and wait for the moment to pass or continue moving forward. It is important to avoid rewarding my dog by allowing them to engage in what they want in that moment (going to meet the kid on the bike, chase the bike, meet the dog, etc.).

It has become a common practice, that I find it concerning is that we allow our dogs to approach others without permission. I often hear statements like, "My dog has to say hi!" or "My dog loves meeting new people/dogs," while their dog pulls on the leash in an excited or anxious state of mind. They allow their dog to enter my safe and private space when I have my dog with me. This is unacceptable. My dog relies on me to protect them and trusts me to handle situations, ensuring they are never placed in uncomfortable positions.

I am actively training my dog to remain neutral around both people and other dogs. Regardless of my dog's training or what is happening between me and my dog, assuming that your dog can approach me, or my dog is impolite. Please teach your dog that they do not *have* to greet everyone they encounter. Equally important, please seek permission before approaching with your dog. It is crucial not to assume that every dog is friendly or healthy (fleas, lice, giardia, worms, or ear mites, etc.). Please do not make assumptions about my dog's desire to interact with your dog. Or…even my desire to meet and talk to you. Depends on the day quite frankly.

Extending the same consideration when interacting with someone else's dog is essential. Whether the dog is wearing a service dog vest or not, asking for permission before approaching and touching someone's dog is always polite.

There is an exception to this rule, which applies to therapy dogs that provide comfort to others. These dogs may be deployed in various settings, such as crisis response, hospitals, schools, and more. To assess the situation, one should read the dog's vest or bandana, which may indicate whether an interaction is encouraged or not. "Friendly Pet Me" is a common badge on therapy dog vests. Additionally, look for eye contact and openness from the handler as cues for engagement. In many cases, therapy dog organizations dispatch multiple teams, each comprising a handler and a dog, all wearing the same vest or bandana. These dogs have undergone specific training to handle the potential stress associated with strangers petting and hugging them. In fact, they genuinely enjoy such interactions as it aligns with their purpose, and they wholeheartedly embrace it.

Just as there are times when I, as a dog owner, may not feel like engaging in conversation with a stranger, there are occasions when my dog feels the same. We cherish our time together, enjoying each other's company while working in harmony. Our connection goes beyond spoken words, rooted in an unspoken understanding and deep bond. Let's honor and respect the preferences of both dogs and their owners, fostering an environment of mutual understanding and appreciation.

Regardless of the situation, asking for permission is always the best policy. Asking is not only respectful but also acknowledges the potential obstacles a dog may have encountered during training or rehabilitation. Some dogs do not desire or need to engage with unfamiliar individuals, and there is nothing wrong with that. It is time to normalize and embrace this concept, starting today. This shift in mindset benefits our dogs.

Chapter 14
Cultivating A True Connection

We must stop thinking our dogs innately know how to "behave" as we want them to without proper communication and training. It is unfair to think a dog knows how to walk on a leash properly (without pulling or over-arousal to stimulation in the environment) without your training, guiding, and practicing. Over and over again. It takes time and consistency. So, spend time to actually train your puppy how to walk on a leash. Training has to align with their development (age). We can only assume an older puppy will have the self-control and focus needed to walk through the pet store if we have adequately worked them up to that point. You cannot expect them to behave going from your house to a busy playground without any work in between.

And what happens is you get frustrated. The dog has no expectations (or at least none that have been consistently practiced), and you start making excuses for your dog. In fact, this is how bad it has gotten... a dog constantly pulls on the leash, coughs, and hacks from the pressure of their flat buckle collar? What do we do? We buy them a vest, so it is more comfortable for them to pull. Seriously? We throw in the towel and accept it. But really, this is a failure of yours. The good news? It is never too late to train. It is never too late to still believe in your dog. It is never too late to make necessary changes to improve your dog's state of mind.

**A disclaimer: short nose dog breeds are often referred to as brachycephalic breeds. These breeds include bulldogs, pugs, boxers, and Boston terriers. Due to their unique facial structure, brachycephalic dogs may experience breathing difficulties and other health issues. It's important for owners of these breeds to be aware of potential health concerns and provide appropriate care for them. Also, if any medical condition would harm a dog to wear a collar around their neck, please do not do so. And if your dog walks nicely on a harness, that is great too. **

But let's tackle how to ensure you do not get to this point.

Three things are key to ensure we train our dogs "correctly" with nothing but respect and fairness while honoring them for who they are.

The Three D's of Dog Training: Distance, Duration, and Distraction are three highly effective elements that play a significant role in shaping our dogs' behavior, improving their obedience, and ensuring successful training outcomes so that your dog is not just "trick" trained. But also, a dog that is genuinely a good citizen in our world and they display polite manners.

1. **Distance:** Distance refers to the physical space between you and your dog during training sessions. It is important to gradually increase or decrease the distance depending on the specific skill or behavior you are working on. Start with shorter distances and gradually increase the space as your dog becomes more comfortable and proficient. For example, teaching commands like "sit" or "stay" begins by standing close to your dog and gradually moving farther away over time. Systematically adjusting the distance can help your dog generalize commands in various contexts and environments.

2. **Duration:** Duration refers to the length of time your dog can perform a behavior or maintain a command. Initially, dogs may have difficulty holding a position or staying focused for extended periods. Begin with short durations and gradually increase the time as your dog gains proficiency and focus. For instance, when teaching the "stay" command, start with a few seconds, and gradually build up to several minutes. Gradually increasing the duration can strengthen your dog's impulse control and patience.

3. **Distraction:** Distraction refers to the presence of external stimuli or environmental factors that may divert your dog's attention away from the training task at hand. Introduce distractions gradually, starting with minimal distractions and gradually increasing the level of challenge. For example, begin training in a quiet and controlled environment and gradually introduce mild distractions like low-level noises or movements. As your dog becomes more skilled and focused, you can gradually expose them to more challenging distractions, such as louder noises, other animals, or unfamiliar environments. By systematically desensitizing your dog to distractions, you help them maintain focus and obedience even in distracting real-life situations.

It is important to remember that each dog is unique, and the progression of distance, duration, and distraction will vary based on their abilities and temperament. Always set realistic goals and progress at a pace that suits your dog's learning capabilities.

While we work on the 3 D's of training, we also must keep in mind the concept of "proofing."

Proofing in dog training refers to the process of gradually exposing and training a dog to perform a desired behavior in various environments, situations, and with different distractions. It involves reinforcing the behavior under different conditions to ensure reliability and generalization. We are giving our dog an opportunity to succeed over and over again.

Here's how proofing works in dog training:

1. Gradually Increase Difficulty: Once your dog consistently performs the behavior in a controlled setting, gradually introduce mild distractions or variations. For example, you can practice the behavior in a slightly busier environment or with low-level distractions, such as toys or gentle noises. Gradually increase the difficulty level as your dog demonstrates proficiency.

2. Vary the Training Locations: Dogs are highly context-dependent learners, so practicing the behavior in different locations and settings is essential as you transition from training in your home to other environments such as parks, streets, or friends' houses. This helps your dog understand that the behavior is expected regardless of the location.

3. Reinforce and Correct: During proofing, continue to reinforce the desired behavior with rewards, praise, or play when your dog performs correctly. If your dog makes a mistake or doesn't respond appropriately, use gentle corrections or redirection to guide them back to the correct behavior. Consistency and clear communication are key.

4. Maintain Consistency: Consistency is vital in proofing. Ensure that everyone involved in the training, including family members or caregivers, follows the same guidelines and cues. This helps your dog understand that the behavior is expected in all situations, regardless of who is present.

5. Regularly Review and Practice: Even after successful proofing, it's important to periodically review and practice the behavior in different environments and situations. This helps maintain the reliability of the behavior over time.

Let me use an example with the command "sit." The first step is naming and rewarding, right? So, they know the word and what specific behavior is linked to it. Once that is established with accuracy (how long that takes will depend on the breed's intelligence and your ability), the mistake is that once something is mastered in the house, people think they are set to go anywhere, and their dog will comply with "sit." I hear repeatedly, "They do this at home with no problem! I don't understand!" You are frustrated and maybe even embarrassed because sometimes we do, whether we want to admit to it, weigh our worth as a dog owner based on how our dog acts around others. The easiest thing to do is make excuses. But I am here to tell you, you don't have to do that anymore. So, when I hear this common frustration, I ask, "Where else have you practiced "sitting" besides in your house?"

You all know the answer to that.

Nowhere. We truly felt that once they knew the word, they would happily agree to perform this skill anywhere.

Uh…nope. Sorry. You do not get off that easy. We must practice and proof each command repeatedly in new situations. We need to set them up to succeed and not fail.

So, once my puppy knows the word "sit" before leaving the house, I still add the 3 D's to this command to continue proofing this command to a higher level of obedience. There is so much we can accomplish before the dog is fully vaccinated.

In addition, it is important to teach two other commands: "stay" and the other is the release word from "stay." The release word can be "OK," "Release," "Go," or any other word of your choice. The key is to be consistent and ensure that every person who interacts with your puppy uses the same word while expecting the same behavior. This consistency in language and expectations helps your puppy understand and respond appropriately to the commands.

When training your puppy, it's important to avoid repeating yourself. Although challenging, repeating commands can teach your puppy that they don't have to respond until they hear it multiple times. Or that you will not even enforce it at all. Instead, say the command once and wait for a response. If your puppy doesn't comply, you can use a treat to lure them into the desired position or gently guide their backside down. Reward them once they are in a sitting position and then give the command "sit" again to reinforce the association between the command and the action. This approach helps your puppy understand that they should respond to the command the first time it is given.

It is always important to progress gradually and in a respectful manner that aligns with their ability to focus based on their age. Practice in the backyard once your puppy has mastered the commands in the house and can handle distractions, duration, and distance. Once they are proficient in the backyard, gradually move to the front yard, then gradually increase the difficulty level by practicing a block away, on a busier road, and outside a park.

Observe your puppy's behavior and attention as you progress to more challenging environments. If they become unfocused or struggle to respond, it's a sign that you may be moving too quickly. In such cases, it's best to go back to the previous level they have mastered and find a middle ground between what they can do and what they find challenging. This allows your puppy to build confidence and skills at a pace that suits their individual needs.

Remember, there is no rush or finish line in training. The goal is to develop a long-term relationship with a balanced and fulfilled dog who demonstrates true obedience, self-control, and good manners. By working through each stage patiently and attentively, you set the foundation for a well-behaved companion.

Do it right.
For them and for you

Chapter 15
Eating Crow

People experiencing homelessness have some of the best-behaved dogs. There, I said it. And you don't have to believe me but start paying attention and seeing it for yourself. Those dogs are the most mentally sound. They have been primed for a balanced life (no anxiety or unrealistic fears). They have an owner that does not coddle them for every little sound heard in the environment. They keep moving forward matter of fact, instilling trust. They are steady in their emotions. There is no other option. They are not showered with expensive crystal collars, luxury beds, and 1000 toys. Their needs are met in order, and most of them are at a proper weight. They are held to high expectations regarding rules, boundaries, and limitations. They get plenty of exercise and mental stimulation during the day and lots of love and affection in the evening.

They walk nicely on a leash and have no reactivity to their environment. They stay put whenever needed without having a meltdown. They feel safe. They are respected and they are honored.

Everything in my being still felt like these dogs were severely disadvantaged. They had to be. Right? But the more and more I let judgments slip away from my inner soul and looked at the facts, the harder and harder it was to pity them. I wanted them all "rescued." I know that is extreme, but I do tend to have extreme thoughts from time to time.

In my experience, some would say dogs owned by a homeless human, a wanderer, you could even say, were calmer and more balanced than so many owned by well-off and well-intentioned people. You never see one suffering from anxiety, fear, aggression, or over-excitement. You can pretty much darn well approach any of them and pet them if you choose. You don't see them pulling on the leash, reactive. Overstimulated. Over threshold.

As it is hard to wrestle with the fact, I should actually feel sorry for them, I no longer do. They provide excellent comfort and companionship for their humans, which is a beautiful thing to witness. And these dogs have been set free with so many behavior issues that advantaged dogs continue to suffer with.

Of course, like anything in life, some dogs are not cared for, and I do not condone anyone not caring for their dog. I am making a generalization that I have found to be true.

I have often found that I am slapped back in the face when I make a judgment. And boy does that sting. This is even hard to admit, but the earliest I remember was in high school. I attended prom a few times in high school, and each time, I found girls or boys that would attend after they graduated high school. They were with their crush, high school sweetheart, or whatever you wanted to call it. I judged. I didn't understand why someone would be dating someone in high school when they had already graduated. Little did I know that my little judgy ass would be attending a high school prom at a different school (so I knew no one) a year after graduating. Honestly, the whole night sucked, and a considerable part of that was because I was so in my head about it. From having social anxiety, to not knowing anyone, I was left staring my judgment in the face. I had become that person. The one I was judging the previous few years. I feel the strong need to defend my petty little thoughts here. I never bullied or was intentionally mean to anyone. I have never had that in me. But my deepest, most personal thoughts, on the other hand, are not always the nicest.

I have faced these same instances over and over in life. I am now cautious about judging because I swear it will come full circle if I do. I will find myself sitting in a huge pile of eating crow. It will be hardly palpable but at least I will have one of my dogs alongside me eating it with me too. If that is not man's best friend, I don't know what it is. To be honest, that is a terrible place to be. But one that I have found has led to self-growth and compassion. A place where I have truly learned about empathy. When I get these thoughts or judgments, I quickly evaluate and try to dismiss them before the fairy godmother shakes her wand and makes it a reality for me too.

Unfortunately, crow is still served on my menu from time to time.

The dog world is full of judgments. Breeders judge other breeders. Trainers judge trainers. Dog owners judge other dog owners.

All too often.

Judgments in the dog world can often be unfair and misguided, particularly regarding breed-specific and size judgments. These are often rooted in stereotypes and personal preferences rather than the dog's individual characteristics. Additionally, behavior judgments can be misguided due to a lack of understanding of a dog's body language or past experiences. It's important to remember that each dog breed has its own unique characteristics and tendencies.

While it's crucial to evaluate each dog individually based on their behavior and personality, it's also helpful to consider the fundamental reason why that breed was originally bred and what their innate "job" is. This can give you a better understanding of what to expect from your companion and how to provide them with the appropriate care and training they need to be able to thrive.

Take note for yourself, explore the truth/facts about something, and then you can decide. Some of the hottest topics that are easily judged are hybrid breeding, prong collars, and owners that let their dogs dwell outside.

All dogs were at some point a mix of other breeds. Ethical and responsible breeders have spent their lives fine tuning, preserving, and improving their lines. We are also reaching a time in society where breeders are intentionally breeding two different pure-bred dogs together. And I have personally seen it done when a well-intentioned responsible breeder (insert myself here) gets it right, and they can in fact be amazing dogs. The beautiful thing is that we can choose whatever breed we want. Whatever temperament we need. And when we carefully do that, we are honoring not only our dogs but also ourselves.

Prong collars can be an effective tool used to communicate correctly with your dog when done **correctly**. Different training tools can be a heated debate - like you are stopped in public and given a tongue-lashing, kind of heated debate. Here is my experience with training tools. Any could be harmful. When used with hate and anger, a collar can hurt a dog. A leash could hurt a dog when used with improper intentions. So could a prong collar. It is the hand and heart behind these tools that make them bad. When used correctly, a prong collar can be *such* an effective way to communicate with a dog because is mimics exactly how his mother corrected him. Or another dog. Yep, we are speaking their language. Pretty powerful. When given a little bump on the prong collar through the leash, you can help disrupt those thoughts they have that will lead to unhealthy behaviors and prevent a whole lot of mess for you and the dog. Imagine it from their point of view. They are finally thankful you can speak their language. Training tools are also something to be heavily considered from dog to dog. Some dogs would never need a prong, and others may even need a remote collar due to behavior problems that could lead to aggression.

Remote collars are also highly effective in communicating with your working dog when they are out in the field, hunting or herding cattle, for example. A little bump, and they know when to go. Two bumps, go the other way, etc. It's like braille and brilliant if you ask me.

Any tool put on a dog to punish or hurt them is wrong. Plain and simple. It is abuse. When used to give an effective consequence fairly and humanely, they have kept dogs from being euthanized, rehomed, or living out a life in isolation because humans genuinely don't know what else to do.

Some dogs have purposely been bred to live outside. One example of that is Livestock Guardian Dog breeds. They were intentionally bred to protect their livestock, land, and home. That is what makes them happy. I have, once again, eaten crow when I experienced this *firsthand*. Our "Farm Dog" is a mixed breed mutt, but is mainly Great Pyrenees (a LGD). I couldn't keep him inside if I wanted to. Unless it is the hot as heck Nevada summer days. Then he is happy to be inside. He is honored and happy to be out protecting his chickens, horses, goats, dogs, and humans. He knows who is supposed to be coming and going and watches over all of us. That is his innate purpose and what he *needs* to do.

Training methods are also highly controversial. People always ask me what "type" of trainer they should hire?

Oh boy, here we go.

My first piece of advice is to use a "balanced" trainer. That means they train based on positive rewards but also understand dog psychology, and in real life, in their pack, there are consequences when rules are broken. A balanced dog trainer is an expert who combines positive reinforcement and correction to teach dogs how to behave appropriately. They treat dogs respectfully, understand their needs and personalities and can utilize various training methods. A balanced training approach combines positive reinforcement with correction to teach appropriate behavior. If you have raised children, you understand this elementary concept. Humans also have rules and laws to follow, and for the most part, there are uncomfortable consequences when we break those rules/laws.

For some reason, it is believed that giving a dog a consequence or correction is abuse.

This is false and has caused far more harm to our dogs than good. Remember, as a canine, their first innate need is rules, boundaries, and limitations. They cannot thrive, feel safe, and be fulfilled if they don't have that. A consequence or correction can be as simple as a "no," clap and then "owning the space". Dogs do not, nor should they be beaten or abused. A consequence could be removal from the situation, play stopped, the toy removed, firm words, firm and fair energy, nonverbal cues, or redirection. This training approach must be tailored to each dog's needs and personality. The goal is cultivating a trusting relationship between the dog and owner, ensuring both parties are happy and fulfilled. A balanced dog trainer values the emotional and physical well-being of the dogs they work with and strives to create a harmonious relationship between them and their owners.

A professional dog trainer can train most any dog. Because they get it. They understand. That is their gift. So, remember, that when you use a dog trainer, they will ensure they can train the dog but most importantly train YOU how to communicate with the dog. It doesn't matter that they can command that presence. It matters that you can. If you have done a board and train and seen your unruly dog comply with ease and were shocked at how well they "listened" only to take them home and have the "same" dog you had before, it is because nothing changed in the relationship between you and your dog.

To promote the well-being of our dogs, let us establish a norm where fair, consistent, and respectful consequences and corrections are seen as essential for their proper development and the cultivation of a positive relationship with them.

Dogs can touch our lives in profound ways, providing healing, love, and unwavering support. Their presence brings comfort and joy that surpasses any human interaction. They offer us unconditional love, acceptance, and emotional connection, reminding us of the best versions of ourselves, even in our darkest days.

To truly honor the power of a dog, it is essential to recognize and appreciate their distinct nature. Dogs are not humans, and it is by embracing their true canine essence that we can forge a deep and meaningful bond. By understanding their instincts, needs, and behaviors, we can provide the guidance and care they require to thrive.

In this journey, it is crucial to remember that our dogs are not mere companions but empowering catalysts for change. They have the ability to uplift our flawed human souls, teaching us important life lessons such as unconditional love, resilience, and the power of living in the present moment. Their impact on us transcends generations, leaving a legacy of love and connection.

So, let us continue to believe in the power of a dog, not by treating them as humans, but by honoring and respecting them for who they truly are. Which are remarkable beings that enrich our lives and inspire us to be better. Together, we can create a world where the transformative power of a dog is celebrated, cherished, and embraced, creating a brighter future for both humans and canines alike.

RAISING THE empowered PUPPY

NAME:

DATE OF BIRTH: GENDER:

BREED:

MICROCHIP NUMBER:

MARKINGS:

DIET:

SUPPLEMENTS:

ALLERGIES:

BREEDER:

CONTACT INFO:

VETERINARIAN:

CONTACT INFO:

VACCINATION RECORDS

AGE: DATE:

VACCINATIONS GIVEN:

AGE: DATE:

VACCINATIONS GIVEN:

AGE: DATE:

VACCINATIONS GIVEN:

AGE: DATE:

VACCINATIONS GIVEN:

AGE: DATE:

VACCINATIONS GIVEN:

AGE: DATE:

VACCINATIONS GIVEN:

RAISING THE empowered PUPPY

PREPARATION PLANS

Puppy-proof their living area!

Shop for necessary supplies (see the checklist)!

Schedule a vet appointment for a puppy wellness exam.

Look into pet insurance!

Make sure everyone in the home has agreed to the same rules and expectations.

Get some sleep!

ZZZZ

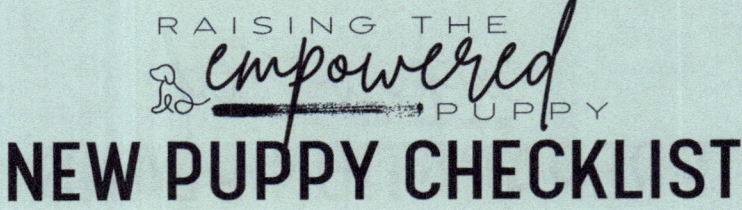

NEW PUPPY CHECKLIST

Scan the QR Code to see a list of our FAVORITE THINGS!

https://www.4ekennels.com/4es-favorites.php

- ☐ Food and water bowls

- ☐ Puppy food (use for treats for now!)

- ☐ Collar and leash

- ☐ Kennel

- ☐ Lifted bed (we love Kuranda)

- ☐ Toys! Choose a variety of safe options. We do not recommend rawhide.

- ☐ Bones! Raw (not cooked), Nyla bones, antlers, etc.

- ☐ Grooming supplies (ear cleaner, brush, comb, shampoo, etc.)
  Items needed will also depend on breed.

- ☐ Poop bags

- ☐ Coupler or hands-free leash for tether training

- ☐ Identification tags or embroidered collar

- ☐ Supplements (we love salmon oil)!

- ☐ Enzyme cleaner for accidents

FAMILY HOUSE RULES

Use this worksheet to help your family make important decisions for your puppy.

Consistency is important for your puppy to be successful.

Where our puppy will sleep:

Our puppy will have access to these areas of the home:

The commands we will use and the expected puppy behavioral outcome (action) include:

Our puppy schedule will be (sample schedule in the 4 week training plan):

Our puppy's designated potty area will be:

The person in charge of the puppy massage and socialization will be:

RAISING THE *Empowered* PUPPY
POTTY TRAINING TIPS

Potty training a puppy can be a challenging but rewarding experience. Here are some tips to help you get started:

» **Establish a routine:** Puppies need to go potty frequently, so establishing a routine will help them learn when and where to go. Take your puppy outside at regular intervals, such as first thing in the morning, after meals, during play, and before bedtime.

» **Use a designated potty area:** Choose a spot outside where you want your puppy to go potty and consistently take them to that spot. Using a designated area will help your puppy associate that spot with going potty.

» **Positive reinforcement:** Praise your puppy when they go potty outside. This will help them learn that going potty outside is a good thing.

» **Supervision:** When your puppy is not in their crate or designated area, keep an eye on them to prevent accidents. If you can't supervise them, confine them to a crate or designated area.

» **Consistency:** Potty training can take several weeks, so be patient and consistent. Stick to your routine and be consistent with praise and positive reinforcement.

» **Clean up accidents promptly:** If your puppy has an accident inside, clean it up promptly with an enzyme cleaner to remove any odor. This will help prevent your puppy from returning to the same spot to go potty.

Remember, potty training takes time and patience. Be consistent and reward your puppy for good behavior, and soon they will be fully potty trained.

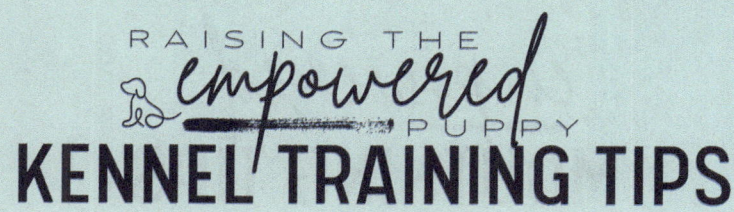

KENNEL TRAINING TIPS

Here are some steps to follow for kennel training your puppy:

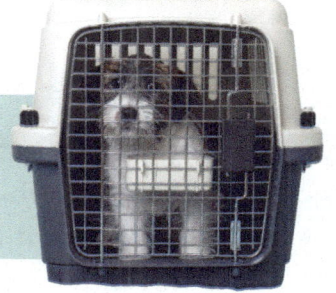

» **Choose the right kennel size:** The kennel should be big enough for your puppy to stand up, turn around, and lay down comfortably. However, it shouldn't be too big, or your puppy may use one end as a bathroom and the other end as a sleeping area.

» **Introduce your puppy to the kennel:** Encourage your puppy to explore the kennel by placing treats or toys inside. Make it a positive experience by offering praise and treats when your puppy goes inside the kennel.

» **Use the kennel for short periods:** Start by having your puppy spend short periods of time in the kennel while you are at home. This will help your puppy get used to being in the kennel without feeling isolated.

» **Take your puppy outside:** When you let your puppy out of the kennel, take them outside to use the bathroom. This will help reinforce good bathroom habits.

» **Use the kennel for sleeping:** Once your puppy is comfortable spending longer periods in the kennel, you can start using it for sleeping at night. Place the kennel in your bedroom so your puppy can still hear and smell you.

» **Don't use the kennel as punishment:** The kennel should be a positive place for your puppy, not a punishment.

Kennel training takes time and patience. Be consistent with your training and offer positive reinforcement when your puppy uses the kennel correctly. With time, your puppy will learn to love their kennel and see it as their safe and comfortable space.

MOUTHING TIPS

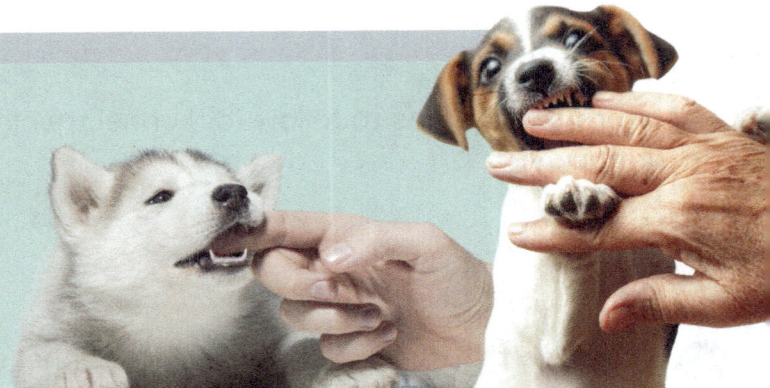

It is natural for puppies to use their mouths and teeth during play and exploration, but it is important to teach them not bite or nip people. Here are some ways to teach your puppy not to bite.

» **Redirect biting behavior:** Whenever your puppy bites you, redirect their attention to a chew toy or another appropriate object to chew on.

» **Remove yourself:** Just remove yourself if they continue mouthing you.

» **Avoid rough play**: Avoid playing games like wrestling, tug-of-war, and keep away with your puppy, as they can encourage biting and nipping behavior.

» **Provide plenty of exercise and playtime:** Puppies need plenty of exercise and playtime to release their energy and reduce the urge to bite or nip.

» **Socialize your puppy:** Socialize your puppy with other dogs and people so they learn to interact appropriately and not use biting or nipping as a means of play or communication.

10-STEP HANDLING EXCERCISES

This approach is performed to improve your puppy's ability to handle different types of touch, handling and sensation. It can be performed in any order. Do not put your puppy down if they are agitated or upset. If they are displaying resistance, stop until the puppy calms and then resume! Reward with positive praise and snuggles when done! However, set your puppy up for success and perform the exercises after all needs have been met and your puppy is getting close to nap time.

1. Cover their eyes.

2. Rub and gently tug on their ears (check for ear cleanliness too!).

3. Open their mouth and inspect their teeth and gums. Have they lost any baby teeth? Are they having any alignment issues?

4. Rub their belly in a wide circular motion.

5. Rub your hand up their back and "heavy" pet. You want to ensure they are not opposed or startled by toddler petting or other heavy petting that may occur at some point in their life.

6. Gently tug and twist on their tail.

7. Rub your fingers in between the pads in their paws.

8. Tap on the tip of their nails (helps desensitize for trimming/cutting).

9. Place your hand around their collar and tug and slide around (no dog should have an aversion to having their collar touched).

10. Touch their nose.

Created and Developed by Jeanette Forrey 2020

RAISING THE
empowered
PUPPY

MEETING THEIR NEEDS IN ORDER

1   RULES, BOUNDARIES AND LIMITATIONS

Puppies thrive with leadership. They want to know what they can and cannot do so that they can live harmoniously with their human(s). They will thrive with consistency and fairness. Some examples include:

- going potty outside
- no mouthing on skin
- no jumping on people
- no chasing the cat

2   MENTAL AND PHYSICAL STIMULATION

Puppies need exercise! And, love to feel proud of things they accomplish (training). Daily walks, short and fun training sessions, brain games, running, playing, sniffing, etc. are some great ways to ensure their mental and physical needs are met.

3   LOVE AND AFFECTION

It is so easy to give love and affection first and foremost, but to meet the needs of your puppy in ORDER, this is done last! To raise a balanced and fulfilled puppy, give love and affection when they are in a calm state of mind. This will reduce the chance of over arousal, over excitement and anxiety.

SAMPLE SCHEDULE

MEETING THEIR NEEDS IN ORDER

SAMPLE MORNING SCHEDULE OF
MEETING THEIR NEEDS IN ORDER

Acvtivity	→	Needs Met
Wake up in a kennel		Rules, boundaries and limitations
Go outside and go potty		Rules, boundaries and limitations
Play fetch, run around and sniff or take a walk		Mental and physical stimulation
Short and fun training session		Mental and physical stimulation
Breakfast time – sitting and waiting calmly!		Mental stimulation
10 Step Handling Exercises		Rules, boundaries and limitations
Massage and cuddling		Love and affection
Nap time in a kennel		Start over with rules, boundaries and limitations!

Repeat!
Keep their needs in mind and not yours!

RAISING THE empowered PUPPY

PUPPY, PUPPY, PUPPY RECALL

TO CONSIDER

If your puppy bolts out into traffic, assess the situation quickly. Calling them might be fatal because you may be asking them to run back into traffic.

If you encounter an aggressive dog, this recall could be great, or it could trigger the aggressive dog to chase (a long down stay might be best in this situation). Again, assess and use your best judgement.

Step it up and practice this command with a long drag line (20 plus feet) and take them out in a high distraction area. When they are not focused on you, call "puppy puppy puppy". If they don't come? Reel them in and keep calling them. Remember to only be positive and happy (even if you are frustrated and have to reel them in). Give them lots of praise and a treat when they reach you. Let them go back out and explore and place and repeat a few times. Coming to you should always be positive and safe!

We imprint all of our puppies to the recall of "puppy puppy puppy". This is a lifesaving tool we are giving you, so what can you do to ensure your puppy continues to have this vital recall?

» Practice twice a week with a high value treat that they never get otherwise (cheese, chicken, hot dog, etc.). Wait for them to be distracted by something (focus is not on you) and then call, "Puppy puppy puppy!" As soon as your puppy gets to you, have the biggest "puppy party" and give them the treat. That's it!

» Do not ever use "puppy puppy puppy" as a punishment (to put them in their kennel, call them from inside, etc.). It must be 100% positive EVERY single time!

» Do not overuse this command. Your dog will learn very quickly to ignore you if this command is overused. Practicing twice a week after 4 weeks of practice is generally sufficient.

» How long should you keep reinforcing this command? We recommend doing this for the rest of your dog's life.

» When can you use this command? If your dog bolts out of the door, won't recall when off leash, and any other potentially dangerous situation.

THE TREAT GAME

Puppies are notorious for picking up everything and anything. Acknowledging that while dogs explore the world through their mouth and nose, this can also be dangerous when they start gulping items or get hold of something poisonous.

Anytime the puppy has something in their mouth they should not, or that you need to get from them, simply call, "treat" and go to the fridge. They will drop the item when you say treat or when they get to you. Do not put any focus on it! Put your foot over it and wait for the pup to toddle off. Then pick it up. Do not ever chase a puppy with something in their mouth. You are only adding value to it. Just call "treat" and walk to the fridge. No panic or stress! You have done your work in ensuring you don't have a resource guarder or gulper in your house!

WEEK 1 Once a day (if possible) wait for your pup to be interested in something else. Walk up to them and put the tasty treat at their nose and say, "treat". Give the pup the treat and praise. That's it!

WEEK 2 Start calling "treat" and have the puppy come to you! No barriers involved. Be in sight. When the puppy comes to you, give them the treat and praise! That's it!

WEEK 3 Call treat and go to the fridge. Barriers and distractions can be at play now. Challenge the pup and wait until they are playing with a toy! Reward with a tasty treat! That's it!

WEEK 4 You only need to do this a few times a week. Wait for the pup to be really interested in something else (another dog, toy, bone, food, children, etc.). Give a high value treat from the fridge and praise them. That's it!

Prevent resource guarding and gulping!

Resource guarding in dogs is a behavior where a dog displays aggressive or defensive behaviors to protect valuable resources, such as food, toys, bones, treats, or even specific locations like beds or resting areas. The dog perceives these items as valuable and feels the need to defend them from perceived threats, which may include other pets, humans, or even unfamiliar stimuli.

RAISING THE empowered PUPPY
SOCIALIZATION TIPS

Socializing a puppy is important to help them become well-adjusted, confident, and happy adult dogs. Here are some tips for socializing your puppy:

- **Introduce your puppy to new people:** Puppies should be introduced to a variety of people of different ages, genders, and ethnicities. Make sure that each interaction is positive, short, and rewarding for your puppy.

- **Socialize your puppy with other dogs**: Dogs are social animals, so it's important for your puppy to interact with other dogs. Puppy training classes and play dates are great ways to socialize your puppy with other dogs.

Remember that socialization is an ongoing process and should continue throughout your puppy's life. By socializing your puppy properly, you can help them become a happy, confident, and well-adjusted adult dog.

- **Expose your puppy to different environments:** Puppies should be exposed to different environments, such as parks and other public areas. This will help them get used to new sights, sounds, and smells.

- **Provide positive experiences:** When socializing your puppy, make sure that each experience is positive and rewarding. Use treats and praise to reinforce good behavior.

- **Gradually increase exposure:** Start with short interactions and gradually increase the duration and intensity of socialization sessions. This will help your puppy build confidence and prevent them from becoming overwhelmed.

RAISING THE *empowered* PUPPY

STRESS SIGNALS

Puppies can display a variety of stress signals when they are feeling anxious, fearful or overwhelmed. Here are some common stress signals in puppies:

It's important to pay attention to your puppy's body language and behavior to identify signs of stress. If your puppy is showing stress signals, try to remove them from the stressful situation or provide them with a calm and safe environment or get them moving forward with play and distraction. Forward movement is a powerful way to manage fear. Do not hold or coddle them, rather empower them. When they reach higher levels of stress and give signals, please watch, listen and honor them.

1. **Yawning:** Puppies may yawn when they are feeling stressed, even if they are not tired.
2. **Panting:** Excessive panting, especially when the puppy is not hot or exercising.
3. **Lip licking:** Puppies may lick their lips when they are feeling anxious or stressed.
4. **Whining or barking:** Puppies may vocalize when they are feeling stressed or uncomfortable.
5. **Pacing or restlessness:** Puppies may pace or wander aimlessly when they are feeling stressed.
6. **Avoidance or withdrawal:** Puppies may try to avoid or withdraw from situations or people that make them feel stressed.
7. **Trembling or shaking:** Puppies may tremble or shake when they are feeling fearful or stressed.
8. **Tail tucking or low carriage:** Puppies may tuck their tail between their legs or carry it low when they are feeling stressed or fearful.
9. **"Whale Eyes":** Puppies may open their eyes wide which results in being able to see the whites of their eyes, known as the sclera.
10. **Growling:** Puppies may growl if their stress level has reached a point where they feel fearful.

HOW WE HANDLE FEAR MATTERS

So what should you do when your puppy experiences an unrealistic fear?

» Stay Neutral/Keep a strong and safe composure.

» Use the "yes" empowerment word.

» Coax the puppy to investigate or at least move on to something else with ease.

» Desensitize with the same object or noise over the next few days using treats/praise.

» Forward movement is powerful! Do not let a dog "sit" in fear. And definitely do not pet or hold a dog in a fearful state of mind. Get out a leash (if not on one already) and get on the move. Be positive and confident!

COMMUNICATION

EFFECTIVELY COMMUNICATING WITH A PUPPY

For the first several weeks, prevent and distract rather than make your puppy think his/her name is "No"! But when a puppy does need to learn the rules and boundaries in your home, follow these steps to ensure you are communicating with your puppy effectively.

» Interrupt the thought BEFORE the undesired behavior happens (a clap and a sharp "no" works well).

» Stand firm and still.

» Wait for the puppy to relent to ensure the message was received. They may leave or look away.

You will have to repeat!
Be 100% consistent!
Be fair and kind!

Remember, the first innate need of a puppy (besides food and shelter) is rules, boundaries and limitations. Puppies feel safer when they have a reliable and fair leader. So lead with respect and fairness.

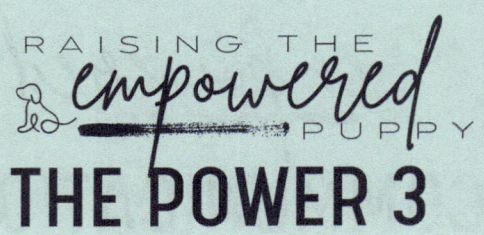

THE POWER 3

SIT ON THE DOG

This is an easy training tip, and it doesn't require you to "sit on your dog" – Rather, place the collar on your puppy and then sit on the leash. Grab some reading material and get comfortable. The goal is to get your puppy to lie at your feet with little tension on the leash.

HAND FEEDING

Hand feeding is an excellent way to build focus and self-control and lay the foundation of nothing in life is for free. You want your puppy to be focused on you! You are the giver, not the taker!

TETHER TRAINING

Tethering your puppy to you teaches manners, keeps your puppy safe and aids in potty training. If they are always tethered to you, you can correct unwanted behavior more effectively. It is much easier to train by expectation than trying to fix unwanted behavior that you missed. It also builds a beautiful innate bond between humans and canine that is connected through the power of a leash. Something safe. And not something that becomes a fight or creates tension.

THE THREE D'S OF TRAINING

There are 3 words that are important to remember when training your puppy. Too often we go from the house to an overstimulating environment. We are only setting our puppies up to fail. We need to pace them in a way that aligns with their social development so they can be successful.

Distance

Distance refers to the physical space between you and your puppy during training sessions. It is important to gradually increase or decrease the distance depending on the specific skill or behavior you are working on.

Duration

Duration refers to the length of time your puppy can perform a behavior or maintain a command. Initially, dogs may have difficulty holding a position or staying focused for extended periods.

Distraction

Distraction refers to the presence of external stimuli or environmental factors that may divert your puppy's attention away from the training task at hand. Introduce distractions gradually, starting with minimal distractions and gradually increasing the level of challenge.

An important thing to remember is that when your puppy breaks a "stay" they need to be returned to where you told them to stay in the first place and try again.

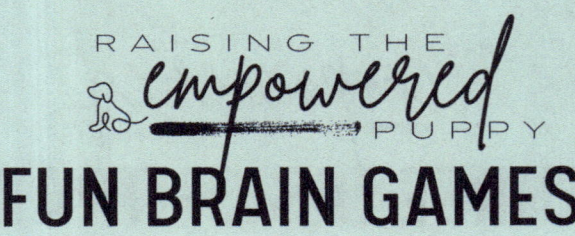

FUN BRAIN GAMES

Remember to always supervise your puppy during brain games and use positive reinforcement to encourage good behavior. These games can help strengthen the bond between you and your puppy and provide mental stimulation that can help reduce destructive or undesirable behaviors.

Playing brain games with your puppy can be a great way to provide mental stimulation and keep them entertained. Here are some fun brain games for puppies:

» **Hide and Seek**: Hide treats around the house or yard and encourage your puppy to find them. Start with easy hiding spots and gradually increase the difficulty.

» **Puzzle Toys:** Puzzle toys, such as treat dispensers or interactive toys, can challenge your puppy's problem-solving skills, and keep them entertained for hours.

» **Name that Toy:** Teach your dog the names of their toys and encourage them to bring you a specific toy when you call it by name.

» **Cup Game:** Place a treat under one of three cups and mix them up. Encourage your dog to find the cup with the treat underneath.

» **Shell Game:** Like the Cup Game, place a treat under one of three cups or small containers and shuffle them around. Encourage your dog to find the treat by following the cup that has the treat.

» **Seek and Sniff:** Hide treats or toys in a specific room or area and encourage your puppy to find them using their sense of smell.

JUMPING TIPS

Jumping on people is a common behavior problem for puppies, but it can be corrected with consistent training and patience.

Here are some steps to teach your puppy not to jump on you:

» Ignore a jumping puppy. Do not praise or touch a puppy jumping on you. When they sit and look at you, acknowledge and reward!

» Walk right back into their space. So easy and effective. It is human nature to use our hands to push them off of us or step backward. Both of those behaviors encourage jumping. Put her your hands on your hips and walk right into them.

» Consistency is key!

With patience and consistency, your puppy can learn to greet people in a calm and polite manner. Do not let any visitors baby talk or pet your puppy when they jump on them. You must teach them to ignore the young puppy until they are calm and all 4 paws are on the floor!

LITTLE PALS AND PUPS

Don't make a peep, let the puppy sleep!

Puppies require a lot of rest. Teach little pals to respect a puppy that is sleeping.

Waking a sleeping puppy can lead to startling, disorientation and even biting.

Freeze like a tree with a jumping puppy!

Stand Still.

Place your hands under your arm pits.

Freeze like a tree.

Keep turning your behind to them.

Sit like a Statue!

Let the puppy dictate play too! Have the child sit on the floor and the puppy gets to come and go and choose the games (no inadvertent teasing by continuously pulling the the toy away).

This Plan will Empower:

....

(Name of your puppy)

RAISING THE empowered PUPPY
SOCIALIZATION CHART

Tag, you're it! It's your turn to work on curriculum and exposure. Make the next 8 weeks of your puppy's life count! Here's a list of suggested ways to empower your puppy through socialization.

PEOPLE

Young (Babies, Toddlers)
Teenagers
Middle-Aged
Elderly
All Skin Colors

PLACES

Vet's Office
Friend's Home
Store
Park (Observe Only)
Park (Meet New People)
Outside a School
Social Gathering
Groomer/Self-Wash
Neighborhood Walk
Outdoor Cafe
Puppy Obedience Class

SURFACES

Slippery/Wet
Uneven/Bumpy
Grates
Decks
Bridges
Tile
Carpet
Wood Floors

TEMPERAMENT

Loud/Confident
Quiet/Timid
Crying/Scared
Deep Voices
High Pitched Voices

MOVING OBJECTS

Cars/Pickup Trucks
Semi-Trucks
Busses
Construction Trucks
Garbage Trucks
Motorcycles
Bicycle/Skateboard
Shopping Carts
Strollers
Wheelchairs
Airplanes

ANIMALS

Stable Adult Dogs
Puppies
Cats/Kittens
Birds/Fowl
Livestock
Horses
Rabbits
Squirrels

ACCESSORIES/ATTIRE

Glasses/Sunglasses
Hats/Helmets
Raincoats/Capes
Walkers/Canes/Crutches
Masks

SOUNDS

Screaming/Shouting
Crying Baby
Fireworks/Gunshots
Clapping
Busy Street
Vacuum
Ice Maker
Blender
Blow Dryer
Garage Door
Lawn Mower
Sirens
Echo
Television
Radio (Different Music)
Thunder
Doorbell
Hammering
Smoke Detector
Alarm
Dogs Barking
Singing

Remember to keep all 4's OFF the floor! Do not let their paws touch the ground until they have been fully vaccinated. (Usually 2 weeks after their 16-week shots, but coordinate with your veterinarian)

Created and Developed by Jeanette Forrey 2020

RAISING THE EMPOWERED PUPPY

WEEK 1 AT HOME

>>> This weekly guide is based on taking home an 8-week-old puppy. Remember that puppies develop at different rates, so adjust the training according to your puppy's progress and individual needs. Additionally, ensure your puppy receives proper veterinary care, vaccinations, and a balanced diet for their overall well-being.

🔍 Weekly Focus

Build a foundation based on respect and trust through firmness, fairness and consistency.

☑ Meet Their Needs In Order

1. Rules, boundaries, and limitations
2. Mental and physical exercise
3. Love and affection

🌿 Environment

Keep your puppy at home and get them settled in. They need to feel safe and comfortable in their new space. The only time our puppies leave in the first week is if they have a vet visit. Reduce the space they are allowed to aid in potty training and unwanted behaviors of chewing and chasing things they should not.

Follow your family house rules with 100% consistency.

🕐 Daily Sample Schedule

	AM Potty
	AM Play
	AM Daily Task Work
	AM Feeding
	AM Potty
	AM Love and Affection
	AM Nap
	PM Potty
	PM Exposure Work
	PM Play
	PM Daily Task Work
	PM Love and Affection
	PM Nap
	PM Feeding
	PM Potty
	PM Play
	PM Love and Affection
	PM Bedtime (in kennel if training)

Daily Tasks

Use their kibble before feeding time to practice some of these foundational tasks I have covered in this book! Check off each task performed each day and make note of 3 socialization exercises completed for the week.

✓ **Daily Check-off**

	S	M	T	W	Th	F	S
NAME GAME: Say their name and reward them for looking at you!	☐	☐	☐	☐	☐	☐	☐
FOLLOW ME: Puppy follows you using the command "let's go" and reward them for following you.	☐	☐	☐	☐	☐	☐	☐
SIT ON THE DOG EXERCISE: Sit on the puppy's leash until the puppy settles at your feet.	☐	☐	☐	☐	☐	☐	☐
FREE PLAY: Let your puppy decide to choose what and how to play. You stay put and they come and go.	☐	☐	☐	☐	☐	☐	☐
TREAT GAME: Practice and reinforce this life-saving command once a day by saying "treat" and reward.	☐	☐	☐	☐	☐	☐	☐
PUPPY PUPPY PUPPY: Say "puppy puppy puppy" and reward them for coming to you!	☐	☐	☐	☐	☐	☐	☐
"YES" EMPOWERMENT WORD: Use the "yes" empowerment word as they are being brave and exploring new things.	☐	☐	☐	☐	☐	☐	☐
10-STEP HANDLING EXERCISES: Make sure this is done when the puppy is in a calm state of mind.	☐	☐	☐	☐	☐	☐	☐

Socialization / Exposure work

Select 3 items from the socialization chart that you can accomplish from the safety of your home.

1.

2.

3.

RAISING THE empowered PUPPY

WEEK 2 AT HOME

>>> Having the first week down, where most of that week was spent on bonding and adjusting, we can now move into some new work for you and your puppy!

Weekly Focus

Continue building a foundation of respect and trust through firmness, fairness and consistency.

Remember to have short and fun training sessions.

Meet Their Needs In Order

1. Rules, boundaries, and limitations
2. Mental and physical exercise
3. Love and affection

Health/Grooming Needs

Make sure you are brushing your new puppy to make grooming later easier for you both!

Continue to handle paws in preparation of nail trims.

Environment

- Continue to make sure all family members are 100% consistent with the rules of the house.

- Take your puppy for some short and fun car rides.

- Introduce a few new people to your puppy this week. Remember to have them ignore your puppy until the puppy chooses to engage first.

- Consider extending your puppy's living space a little bit.

Reminders

- To prevent mischievous puppy behavior, it's important to modify their environment and remove items such as shoes, toilet paper, and grass that they could ruin or chew on.

- When puppies are bored, they tend to engage in excessive chewing behavior.

- Lastly, if your puppy starts mouthing on you, it's essential to disengage from the play and redirect their attention to prevent further mouthing.

WEEK 2 DAILY TASKS

Daily Tasks

Use their kibble before feeding time to practice some of these foundational tasks! Check off each task performed each day and make note of 3 socialization exercises completed for the week.

✓ Daily Check-off

	S	M	T	W	Th	F	S

NAME GAME & FOLLOW ME: Continue saying their name and reward them for looking at you. Use the command "let's go" and reward them for following you (do this with and without them dragging the leash). ☐☐☐☐☐☐☐

SIT ON THE DOG EXERCISE: Sit on the puppy's leash until the puppy settles at your feet. Practice in different locations around the house. ☐☐☐☐☐☐☐

FREE PLAY: Let your puppy decide to choose what and how to play. You stay put and they come and go. ☐☐☐☐☐☐☐

TREAT GAME: Practice and reinforce this life-saving command once a day by saying "treat" and reward. ☐☐☐☐☐☐☐

PUPPY PUPPY PUPPY: Say "puppy puppy puppy" and reward them for coming to you! ☐☐☐☐☐☐☐

"YES" EMPOWERMENT WORD: Use the "yes" empowerment word as they are being brave and exploring new things. ☐☐☐☐☐☐☐

10-STEP HANDLING EXERCISES: Make sure this is done when the puppy is in a calm state of mind. ☐☐☐☐☐☐☐

SIT & COME: Introduce basic commands such as "sit" and "come." Use their kibble before feeding and positive reinforcement to encourage your puppy to follow these commands. ☐☐☐☐☐☐☐

Socialization / Exposure work

Select 3 items from the socialization chart that you can accomplish from the safety of your home.

1.

2.

3.

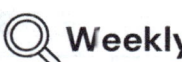

WEEK 3 AT HOME

>>> Week 3 is exciting since most puppies will receive their last set of vaccines this week (if you took them home at 8 weeks old). Once a puppy has completed their puppy vaccines, you are able to expand their exposure work. Please check with your veterinarian for when this will be.

🔍 Weekly Focus

Continue building a foundation of respect and trust through firmness, fairness and consistency while adding distraction and new locations. Remember to have short and fun training sessions, while watching for any stress signals.

☑ Meet Their Needs In Order

1. Rules, boundaries, and limitations
2. Mental and physical exercise
3. Love and affection

➕ Health/Grooming Needs

Around 11-12 weeks old, your puppy will need another set of vaccines. Check with your veterinarian.

It may be time to make a grooming appointment for when they turn 16 weeks old and are fully vaccinated. Expose them to the blow dryer and other grooming tools.

🍃 Environment

- Take longer and more productive car rides now that your puppy has been exposed to the car.
- Always bring a high-value treat for them on a ride! Make it positive and fun!
- Let them smell and see the world from the safety of the window. Can you drive around a busy parking lot and let them experience the world in a safe manner.
- Introduce a few new people to your puppy. Remember to have them ignore your puppy until the puppy chooses to engage first.
- Consider extending your puppy's living space some.
- Expand socialization to include other dogs, gradually introducing them in controlled environments.

🔔 Reminders

- Continue to make sure all family members are 100% consistent with the rules of the house
- When puppies are bored, they tend to engage in excessive chewing behavior.
- If your puppy starts mouthing on you, it's essential to disengage from the play and redirect their attention.
- A good groomer will take their time to expose your puppy to the dryer, grooming table, etc.

WEEK 3 DAILY TASKS

Daily Tasks

Use their kibble before feeding time to practice some of these foundational tasks! Check off each task performed each day and make note of 3 socialization exercises completed for the week.

✓ Daily Check-off

	S	M	T	W	Th	F	S
NAME GAME & FOLLOW ME: Continue saying their name and reward them for looking at you. Use the command "let's go" and reward them for following you (do this with and without them dragging the leash).	☐	☐	☐	☐	☐	☐	☐
SIT ON THE DOG EXERCISE: Sit on the puppy's leash until the puppy settles at your feet. Practice in different locations around the house.	☐	☐	☐	☐	☐	☐	☐
FREE PLAY: Let your puppy decide to choose what and how to play. You stay put and they come and go.	☐	☐	☐	☐	☐	☐	☐
TREAT GAME: Practice and reinforce this life-saving command once a day by saying "treat" and reward.	☐	☐	☐	☐	☐	☐	☐
PUPPY PUPPY PUPPY: Say "puppy puppy puppy" and reward them for coming to you!	☐	☐	☐	☐	☐	☐	☐
"YES" EMPOWERMENT WORD: Use the "yes" empowerment word as they are being brave and exploring new things.	☐	☐	☐	☐	☐	☐	☐
10-STEP HANDLING EXERCISES: Make sure this is done when the puppy is in a calm state of mind.	☐	☐	☐	☐	☐	☐	☐
GROOMING EXPOSURE: Make sure to give your puppy a bath and blow-dry session once this week, and on a daily basis, spend some time brushing them while introducing them to a brush, comb, nail clippers, and other grooming tools.	☐	☐	☐	☐	☐	☐	☐
SIT, COME, DOWN & SAY: Introduce basic commands such as "down" and "stay." Use treats and positive reinforcement to encourage your puppy to follow these commands. Keep practicing sit and come.	☐	☐	☐	☐	☐	☐	☐

Socialization / Exercise work

Select 3 items from the socialization chart that you can accomplish from the safety of your home.

1.

2.

3.

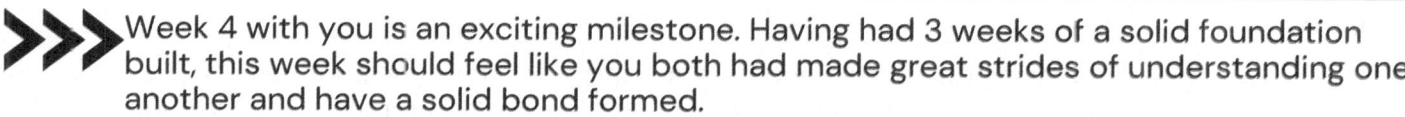

WEEK 4 AT HOME

>>> Week 4 with you is an exciting milestone. Having had 3 weeks of a solid foundation built, this week should feel like you both had made great strides of understanding one another and have a solid bond formed.

🔍 Weekly Focus

Continue building a foundation of respect and trust through firmness, fairness and consistency while adding distraction and new locations.

Remember to have short and fun training sessions, while watching for any stress signals.

☑ Meet Their Needs In Order

1. Rules, boundaries, and limitations
2. Mental and physical exercise
3. Love and affection

➕ Health/Grooming Needs

Week 4 marks an important landmark for your puppy as they should have received their full vaccinations (please consult your veterinarian to confirm this).

Keep brushing your puppy and practicing grooming type handling and exposure.

🌿 Environment

- It is time to do short and fun exposure work (some puppies can only do 5 minutes at a time so watch for stress signals) outside of the home. Start with less busy places and work toward more unpredictable places. Remember, you are still building trust.
- Reward neutral and calm behavior. We don't want reactive dogs.
- Meet new people this week!
- Consider giving puppy supervised freedom in more areas of your home.
- Continue to make sure all family members are 100% consistent with the rules of the house.
- Continue socialization with other dogs, gradually introducing them in controlled environments.

🔔 Reminders

- The specific vaccines required may vary depending on your location and the recommendations in your area. Additionally, depending on where you live, it may be necessary to provide your puppy with flea and tick medication before taking them outdoors. It is crucial to seek guidance from your veterinarian regarding your puppy's overall health and well-being.

Daily Tasks

Typically since we are increasing distraction and duration this week in training, we need treats! Continue to take the time to practice some of these foundational tasks! Check off each task, and make note of 3 socialization exercises completed for the week.

✓ **Daily Check-off**

	S	M	T	W	Th	F	S

NAME GAME & FOLLOW ME: Continue saying their name and reward them for looking at you and using the command "let's go" and reward them for following you (do this holding the leash). ☐ ☐ ☐ ☐ ☐ ☐ ☐

SIT ON THE DOG EXERCISE: Sit on the puppy's leash until the puppy settles at your feet. Practice in different locations outside in your front and back yard/patio. ☐ ☐ ☐ ☐ ☐ ☐ ☐

TETHER TRAINING: If puppy is ready to start tether training, please see the handout that explains this important exercise or find the link to the video at the end of these handouts. ☐ ☐ ☐ ☐ ☐ ☐ ☐

TREAT GAME & PUPPY PUPPY PUPPY: You can now practice these life-saving commands 2-3 times a week. ☐ ☐ ☐ ☐ ☐ ☐ ☐

"YES" EMPOWERMENT WORD: Use the "yes" empowerment word as they are being brave and exploring new things. ☐ ☐ ☐ ☐ ☐ ☐ ☐

10-STEP HANDLING EXERCISES: Make sure this is done when the puppy is in a calm state of mind. ☐ ☐ ☐ ☐ ☐ ☐ ☐

SIT, COME, DOWN, STAY & add WAIT, DROP IT & LEAVE IT: Introduce these new commands. Use treats and positive reinforcement to encourage your puppy to follow these commands. Keep practicing, sit, come, down, and stay. Mix up the order you ask your puppy to perform these tasks. ☐ ☐ ☐ ☐ ☐ ☐ ☐

Socialization / Exposure work

Select 3 items from the socialization chart that you can accomplish from the safety of your home.

1.

2.

3.

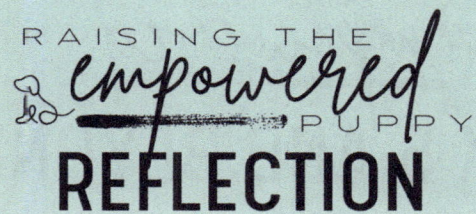

REFLECTION

Let's reflect on how the last 4 weeks have gone!

Focus

Do you feel you have started a bond built on respect and trust?

Environment /Daily Schedule

Do you feel your puppy has a solid understanding of their schedule, kennel training and potty training?

Socialization and Exposure Work

Any concerns or unrealistic fears to work on?

Commands

Rate the consistency your puppy follows these commands at the end of your 4 weeks:

Sit seldom /sometimes / most of the time

Down seldom /sometimes / most of the time

Stay seldom /sometimes / most of the time

Come seldom /sometimes / most of the time

Wait seldom /sometimes / most of the time

Drop It seldom /sometimes / most of the time

Leave It seldom /sometimes / most of the time

Daily Tasks

Were you able to fit in each recommended task?

What task does your puppy enjoy the most?

What task has been the biggest challenge?

Reminder:

It's important to make the "come" command enjoyable and rewarding for them. When you introduce more distance and distractions, it can be helpful to have them on a long lead and gradually reel them in while continuously praising them which ensures they don't have the chance to fail. A reliable come command can take up to a year or more for a dog to be truly proficient.

Meet Their Needs In Order

Are you meeting the needs of your puppy in order?

Where do you excel?

Where can you improve?

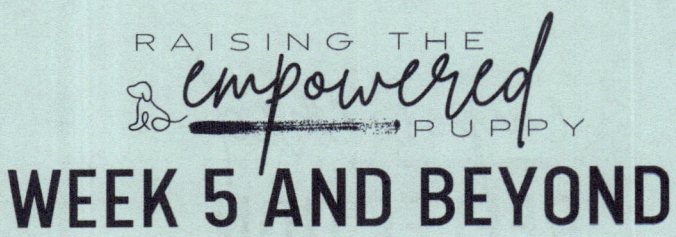

WEEK 5 AND BEYOND

Week 5 and Beyond

Congratulations on the fantastic progress you've made with your puppy over the past four weeks! You've done an incredible job building a strong bond based on trust and respect while also meeting their needs and maintaining a safe, fun, fair, and consistent environment.

Remember to enjoy the training sessions, as puppies grow up so quickly.

As you continue training, focus on enhancing their abilities to stay focused for longer durations, respond from greater distances, and remain unfazed by various distractions.

It's important to keep in mind that every puppy is unique, and their progress may vary. Patience and consistency are key, along with the use of positive reinforcement techniques throughout the training process. Additionally, be sure to create a stimulating environment that also meets the innate needs of the breed of your puppy.

RAISING THE empowered PUPPY

VIDEO RESOURCES

Here are some video resources to help you through the first year of puppy raising:

For New Puppy Owners

**The Power 3 Series
(sit on the dog, hand feeding
and tether training)**

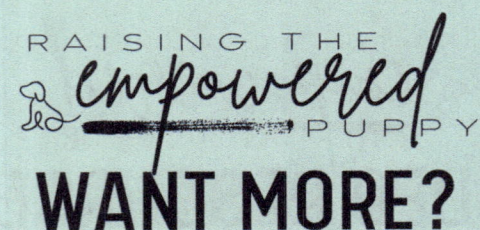

WANT MORE?

Check out this amazing online puppy school resource that we love!

https://www.baxterandbella.com/
Use Discount Code: empoweredpuppy to receive 25% off

25% OFF

https://youtube.com/@4EKennels
Subscribe to our YT Channel for informational videos.

https://www.facebook.com/4ekennelsbadassbreeder
Follow us on Social Media for more empowering tips!

https://www.instagram.com/4ekennels/
Follow us on Social Media for more empowering tips!

https://www.buzzsprout.com/1965053
Listen to our Podcast on Apple, Amazon, Spotify, iHeart Radio and more!

FOR ME, SHARING THE POWER OF A *dog* IS LIFE CHANGING AND INCREDIBLY REWARDING!

— JEANETTE FORREY —

Made in the USA
Las Vegas, NV
17 February 2025

18271740R00072